Formula One

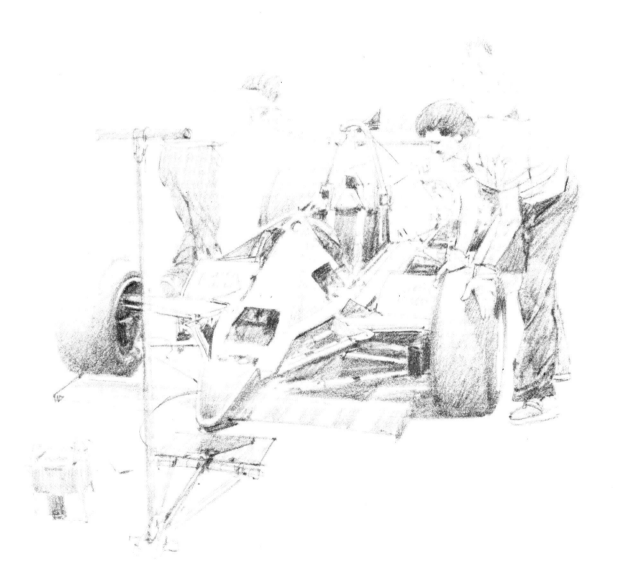

*Ascari squeezes through the first lap wreckage
in the 1950 Monaco Grand Prix*

Formula One

the Cars and the Drivers

Paintings by Michael Turner
Commentary by Nigel Roebuck

TEMPLE PRESS

To Helen

Published by Temple Press
an imprint of Newnes Books
Astronaut House, Feltham, Middlesex, England
and distributed for them by
The Hamlyn Publishing Group Limited
Rushden, Northants, England.

© Artwork copyright Michael Turner 1983
© Text copyright Newnes Books, a division of
The Hamlyn Publishing Group Limited, 1983

First published 1983
ISBN 0 600 35028 2
Printed in Italy

Contents

Foreword

It hardly seems possible that I saw my first motor race in June 1947. I was 14 years old, and on holiday in the Isle of Man with my parents and sisters, our visit coinciding by chance with the running of the revived British Empire Trophy Race. Curiosity took us to an evening practice session, and, from the moment the first E.R.A. blasted past, the thrill and excitement of the world of racing cars fired my imagination, and I was committed to a lifetime attempting to encapsulate and record my visual impressions of the sight and sound of motor racing on paper and canvas.

In those immediate post-war years, when the sport was getting under way again, I cajoled my long-suffering parents into taking me to as many events as possible, setting off at dawn to get a good place at the front of the crowd – the first-ever meetings at Silverstone and Goodwood led to regular pilgrimages, along with Brands Hatch, various hillclimbs, and road races in Jersey as well as return visits to the Isle of Man. Later I was able to make my own way and leave my parents in peace to enjoy quieter pursuits. To them I owe a great debt as they not only indulged my passion, but did all they could to foster and encourage my aspirations to follow a career in art – a dubious course in many people's eyes, but even more limited given my determination to specialise in painting and drawing cars, particularly racing cars, and aircraft.

My endeavours were rewarded whilst I was still a student, with drawings appearing in *Motor* and the BARC Gazette, which led on to my first track pass at Goodwood, paintings being shown at the old Steering Wheel Club in London, and, in 1956, my first commission for Esso. Since those early days, I have devoted a large slice of my life to the portrayal of the sport which has provided me with much motivation, and has taken me to most of the major racing circuits throughout Europe, North and South America, Canada and South Africa. I have shared the cameraderie of the motor racing Press, particularly the photographers, and enjoyed the friendship of many of the drivers as well as their entrants and sponsors. That I have been able to enjoy a happy home and family life is a considerable credit to my wife Helen, who, like my parents before, has taken an active interest in my enthusiasm and put up with my frequent abscences.

The majority of this book has been compiled from existing work, produced over the years since I became a freelance artist in 1957, but several are new studies, mostly from the 1950s, and I am grateful to the Publishers that I have at last had an excuse to delve into my early memories of Alfas and Ferraris at Silverstone, the might of Mercedes, the beautiful 250F Maserati, and many more, and to reconstruct some of the events which I followed avidly in the pages of the motoring journals at the time.

Regrettably, the days when I travelled with a sketch book and produced 'on the spot' drawings for *Motor* and the BARC Gazette ended in the mid-1960s, a casualty of economics and the facility of the camera as an 'aide memoire'. The production of the drawings which accompany the paintings in this book from my archives and notes has also provided me with great deal of enjoyment, and justifies the observation of some of the fascinating aspects of the motor racing scene which do not necessarily warrant a full painting, but are such an integral part of 'The Circus'. I hope they also acknowledge the hard work of mechanics, teams and officials, who make motor racing possible by their enthusiasm and dedication.

The foundations of Nigel Roebuck's passion for motor racing were also laid in his schooldays. I am delighted that his enthusiasm for the sport, allied with his acknowledged talent for the written word, now complements my efforts.

My thanks are also due to those who have agreed to the inclusion of hitherto unpublished paintings, to the drivers, teams, entrants, sponsors and individuals who now own the originals of most of the other pictures for helping me to remain solvent by their patronage, and to the many kind people who helped me to 'make a go of it' by their encouragement in those early days.

MT

Introduction

My crisis day at school was always Saturday, because the post that morning brought *Autosport,* religiously dispatched by my mother the day before. If the GPO let me down – a rare occurrence in those classless mail days – the weekend was a total loss. It meant waiting until Monday, when we played boy soldiers all afternoon and there was little time to read the latest Grand Prix report or whatever.

In 1961 I responded to an advertisement in the magazine for some motor racing Christmas cards, the work of a man named Michael Turner. And when my cards arrived I was loath to waste them on other people's mantelpieces, instead dashing out to buy the usual stuff with holly and robins and Wise Men. In the end some of the racing cards went out as well, but not those of the Ferraris at Spa. They stayed in my locker, and I have been a devotee of Michael Turner's work ever since.

Now, with this book, we seem to have come full circle. I work as Grand Prix Editor for the magazine which blighted my scholastic career, and Michael continues to capture the essence of the sport like no other artist. Over the years we have met in various parts of the globe, and I was delighted when the publishers suggested that we collaborate on a book.

First of all, it was necessary to establish terms of reference. In addition to his countless paintings of Grand Prix cars, Michael has produced many memorable sports car racing scenes. Being an aficionado of American oval racing, I was also reluctant to omit another of his canvasses which is a particular favourite, that of Jimmy Clark leading A. J. Foyt at Indianapolis in 1965.

In the end, however, we decided that the book should be confined to Grand Prix racing from 1950, the year of the first World Championship. That done, the next task was to work through a vast number of paintings, selecting and discarding, and this was not the work of a moment. By and large, we were in agreement on the choice, although inevitably there were occasions when Michael, especially fond of a particular painting, would express his keenness that it be included, while I would argue that the subject matter was not sufficiently momentous to justify it. And vice versa!

Ultimately, though, I hope we have come up with a fair mix of brilliant art and 'great days'. Some of the paintings in this book have been seen before, as cards or prints, but several are in the hands of private collectors, for many Grand Prix drivers rightly consider the decoration of their houses incomplete without a work by Turner depicting a favourite triumph. In addition, Michael has produced many entirely new paintings and drawings for the book.

It is perhaps inevitable that a degree of prejudice has crept in. This is not wholly a book dealing with success, for there are many defeats more glorious than victories. History books have no taste for emotion and legend, and it is on these that motor racing feeds. I have always felt that raw statistics deal harshly with some, flatter others. Is it true that only winning counts for anything? Not in my world.

Where possible, I have used interview material to revive memories of a particular day, and I rejoice that I have never wiped clean any of the tapes recorded over the years. In my time of reporting Grand Prix racing, Chris Amon and Gilles Villeneuve were particular friends, and if I have drawn upon their words more than most I hope the reader will understand.

NSR

Berne 1950

Farina? Ah, loco, loco ... *I never understood how he survived so long. On the track he was not too bad, but on the road he was a madman. I hated having to drive with him on the way to a race. I was not surprised when I heard that he died in a road accident – only that it did not happen earlier ...*

This was Juan Manuel Fangio recalling his team-mate at Alfa Romeo in 1950 and 1951. When Fangio joined the team, Dr Giuseppe Farina was already comfortably installed as number one driver. Arrogant and aloof, the Italian went back a long way with Alfa Romeo. He had driven for them before the Second World War, and took very seriously his position in the Grand Prix hierarchy. The 1950 season brought with it the inaugural World Championship, comprising six Grands Prix and – for reasons never truly understood – the Indianapolis 500. Farina was determined that the new title should be his, and there seemed little to keep him from his ambition.

In 1950 the Ferrari team was rising, if not yet truly able to challenge Alfa Romeo. Farina's team-mate was to be Luigi Fagioli, still a very fine driver, but now 52 years old and no real threat. That came only when Fangio arrived.

Very quickly the Argentine established himself as a faster driver than Farina, and this the veteran inevitably resented, although he rarely acknowledged it.

The Italian won the opening Grand Prix, at Silverstone, and Fangio won the Monaco Grand Prix the following weekend. A fortnight later they were at the spectacular Bremgarten road circuit for the Swiss Grand Prix.

After practice it was evident that the two men were in a race on their own, even Fagioli being three seconds slower. From the start the three supercharged 158s led easily, with sometimes Fangio, sometimes Farina, in the lead. Towards the end of the race they had lapped everyone else, but any question of a battle to the line disappeared when Fangio retired with a broken valve, leaving Farina to drive on to his second victory.

The Belgian and French Grands Prix both fell to Fangio, but he retired at Monza, the last event of the season, and Farina's win there decided the World

*BRMs at Barcelona
for the 1950 Spanish Grand Prix*

Farina leads Fangio, 1950 Swiss Grand Prix

Championship. Each driver counted his four best scores, and Farina and Fangio had three victories apiece. The issue was settled by the Italian's third place at Spa in the Belgian Grand Prix.

Farina, the beautiful stylist, head back and arms straight even in the cramped cockpits of 1950, never repeated his triumph, although he remained a Grand Prix driver until 1955. He lost his life in 1966 when his Lotus-Cortina went off the road as he travelled to the French Grand Prix.

Silverstone 1951

Froilan Gonzales is a man easily overlooked in the history of this sport, for his career in Grand Prix racing was short, and he won only two World Championship Grands Prix, both of them, remarkably, at the same circuit: Silverstone.

After an indifferent first season in Europe, the burly Argentine returned in 1951, again to drive Maseratis sponsored by his country's Automobile Club. At Reims for the third major race of the season he was approached by Ferrari and asked to stand in for Serafini, who had been hurt in the Mille Miglia.

A distinguished performance at Reims – second, his car taken over by Ascari in the late stages – was enough to persuade Enzo Ferrari to put Gonzales on contract, and his first race as a fully-fledged Ferrari works driver was the British Grand Prix.

At this time Maranello was involved in a struggle to break Alfa Romeo domination, and the two teams were, mechanically, very evenly matched: Ferrari's 4.5-litre unsupercharged engine versus Alfa's 1.5-litre blown unit, each giving around 400 horsepower. On the driving front, though, Ferrari were in trouble.

*Officials extinguish a fire
in Farina's Alfa Romeo, 1951 British Grand Prix*

Alfa Romeo refuelling stop

Alberto Ascari desperately needed another topliner to help him take on the might of Fangio and Farina. Gonzales, it seemed, might be the man.

Shy and humble, Froilan was a little overawed by his new responsibilities, but took to Silverstone immediately, in practice lapping two seconds faster than Ascari! Sandwiched between them, on the front row of the grid, were the Alfas of Fangio and Farina. A huge crowd watched, including members of the Royal Family. The weather was warm and dry. At the back of the grid were the two V16 BRMs of Parnell and Walker, neither of which had practised . . .

Gonzales (12) and Fangio (2) about to lap a Talbot, 1951 British Grand Prix

Gonzales was intensely nervous before the start, but quickly established himself in the lead, driving with flair and confidence, pitching the huge Ferrari sideways and steering it effortlessly on the throttle. It was at once breathtaking and highly efficient.

By the tenth lap Fangio had brought his Alfa right up to the tail of the Ferrari, and quickly he moved through to take over first place. *I knew,* Gonzales recalls, *that it would be easy to make a mistake under pressure from Juan, and there was plenty of time. I let him through and put the pressure on him. I was more comfortable that way . . .*

For 30 laps the two red cars circulated together, never more than a second apart, and Froilan's confidence began to grow. He repassed the Alfa Romeo, the two Argentines now almost a minute clear of any opposition. After the tyre and fuel stops, Gonzales had a lead of more than 20 seconds – despite taking the time to offer his car to Ascari, who had retired earlier!

By the end, the Ferrari was 50 seconds ahead of the Alfa, and Gonzales came in to score a sensational first victory. Tears streamed down his cheeks at the sound of his country's National Anthem, which had been readied for yet another Fangio triumph. For nearly three hours he had opposite-locked his way round Silverstone, always close to the limit, sometimes over it. Not elegant, perhaps, but mightily effective.

Pescara 1951

Alfa Romeo and Ferrari were the only truly competitive teams in Formula 1 in 1951, and both necessarily concentrated most of their efforts on the Championship Grands Prix, taking in non-championship races only when it was convenient. For a decent event, therefore, a race organiser needed both – or neither. If only one materialised, a farce would ensue, and the Pescara Grand Prix was one such. Scuderia Ferrari arrived with three cars, for Ascari, Villoresi and Gonzales, but Alfa Romeo decided against the idea, leaving Juan Manuel Fangio in the role of spectator for the weekend.

The Ferraris faced little in the way of opposition, as the starting grid showed: Ascari inevitably took pole position on the majestic 25.4-kilometre (15.8-mile) road circuit, with Villoresi next to him, but Louis Chiron's Talbot, third fastest, was some 40 seconds from the Italian cars . . .

To avoid the worst of the August sun, the race was started at 9.45 in the morning, and Ascari took an immediate lead, only to retire on the first lap with falling oil pressure. Villoresi came by in first place, shadowed by Gonzales. There was then silence for a little over a minute before Louis Rosier's Talbot arrived, with Chiron's similar car on his tail . . . It was going to be a very long race.

Villoresi came in for tyres at the end of his fourth lap, at which point Ascari took over the car. But that Ferrari, too, expired in Alberto's hands, this one with broken transmission. Gonzales was left with an enormous lead, disappointing for one of his enormous brio and competitiveness, for he was always a man who relished a battle. It was frustrating, too, for Fangio, who stationed himself in the mountains, and hurled cold water at his overheated fellow countryman . . .

The 46-year-old Rosier was never considered to be anything more than a journeyman, but his best days were those when he drove the big, blue Talbots, and at Pescara he overshadowed the cars of Chiron and Phillippe Etancelin, even if utterly unable to challenge Gonzales. At the end of an apparently interminable 12 laps, the stocky Argentine had a lead of more than seven minutes, despite stroking along for most of the morning. If the Alfas had been present, there might have been a race . . .

Ascari and Taruffi on a back stretch at Syracuse, 1952

Syracuse 1952

March 16, 1952 saw the beginning of Alberto Ascari's two-year reign over Grand Prix racing, for it was the date of the Syracuse Grand Prix which traditionally opened the new season. Over the winter the sport's governing body had decided that, until the introduction of the new 2.5-litre Formula 1 in 1954, all Grands Prix should be run to the existing Formula 2, which had a capacity limit of 2 litres. Ferrari, with their new Tipo 500, were all ready to go, and only rarely were they headed in 1952 and 1953.

The brilliant Ascari started as he meant to go on, putting his car on pole position at Syracuse, taking the lead immediately and staying in front for the entire 323 kilometres (201 miles). Such was the pattern of the time. The Italian took part in 15 Formula 1 races in 1952, and won 11 of them. Ferrari were usually without serious opposition, but Alberto was unquestionably the best driver in the team.

Three more factory cars were entered for Syracuse, these assigned to Giuseppe Farina (hired by the Commendatore after the withdrawal of Alfa Romeo), Luigi Villoresi and Piero Taruffi. The only drama to befall the team was that Villoresi's car suddenly caught fire on the starting grid, thanks to some fuel which had been spilled near the exhaust. As a Ferrari mechanic worked away with a fire extinguisher, the race starter dropped his flag . . .

After everyone else was long gone, Villoresi was able to get on his way, climbing to seventh by the end of the race. No one was able to challenge Ascari, although Farina and Taruffi ran in close company for most of the way. On the last lap, indeed, Taruffi incurred the wrath of the good Doctor's many fans when he overtook Farina at virtually the final corner. There were no team orders at Ferrari in those days, but there was – in Farina's eyes, anyway – such a thing as *noblesse oblige*. Having no alternative, he could accept defeat from Ascari, but did not take kindly to presumptuous behaviour from those he considered his inferiors . . .

In the absence of any works Maseratis at Syracuse, Ascari was never under threat, and the same proved to be the case in the Grands Prix (Syracuse was a non-championship race). Opting to take part in the Indianapolis 500 that year, Alberto missed the opening World Championship race, at Berne, but he won all the others.

As ever, the crowd at Syracuse was enormous, thickly spread around the fast 5.5-kilometre (3.4-mile) open road circuit, and the people went home happy for they had seen a Ferrari win. Fifteen years later the last Grand Prix was run there, with Mike Parkes and Lodovico Scarfiotti staging a dead heat, and there was more wild celebration. When it came to Ferraris, no one was more Italian than a Sicilian.

Reims 1953

The French Grand Prix of 1953 has become something of a cliché in racing history, inevitably included – like the Mille Miglia of '55 or the German Grand Prix of '57 – in any anthology of the sport. The nuts and bolts of the affair are that Hawthorn and Fangio battled for a long, long way, with the Englishman finally coming out on top.

Primary requisites for Reims were always a very strong engine and a very brave driver. With the exception of the dauntingly fast right-hander after the pits, there were no corners at this Champagne triangle to tax a driver of real class. But Reims was exceedingly fast, even for the Grand Prix cars of 1953, which had a maximum of 200 horsepower.

For the French Grand Prix each of the major Italian teams fielded four cars; the Ferraris of Ascari, Farina, Villoresi and Hawthorn facing the Maseratis of Fangio, Gonzales, Marimon and Bonnetto. A variety of Coopers, Gordinis, HWMs and Connaughts completed the 27-car field, but none was likely to figure in the race, despite the fact that Jean Behra's Gordini had won at Reims a year earlier.

Mike Hawthorn, in his first season with Ferrari, was very much the junior member of the team, and in

practice he was the slowest of the Maranello quartet. To no one's surprise, the almost unbeatable Ascari took pole position. As the hour of the race neared, however, there was some doubt that there would be any Ferraris in the Grand Prix at all. In the preceding 12-hour sports car race, which traditionally finished at noon on Sunday, the factory Ferrari had been disqualified, and there was some question of the Commendatore's withdrawing his cars from the Grand Prix. Fortunately for motor racing folklore he decided against the idea.

Gonzales took the lead at the start. The Argentine's Maserati was running with only half a tank of fuel, and

would have to stop. It was a gamble, and in the early stages it seemed a worthwhile one. He simply left the rest behind, extending his lead by a full second each lap, but it was not quite enough. At the halfway point he came in for fuel, and dropped to sixth, behind Fangio, Hawthorn, Ascari, Farina and Marimon. In a matter of seven laps, however, Gonzales was fourth and pushing Ascari.

As the race went into its final 20 laps it became increasingly obvious that Hawthorn was the only Ferrari driver able to challenge Fangio seriously. Their cars were evenly matched, the Maserati's slight power

1953 Formula One Gordini

advantage balanced by the Ferrari's superior road-holding and brakes. That being the case, it was logical that the experience of Fangio would win the day.

But the great man had a problem: *Soon after the halfway mark I found that I could not get first gear, which I needed for the very slow Thillois hairpin at the beginning of the pit straight. It was not easy to disguise the fact from Hawthorn . . .*

With a few laps left Mike spotted the Maserati's defect. As they went into their final lap the Ferrari led over the line, but Fangio repassed on the long straight down to Thillois. At the approach to the corner Hawthorn went for the inside, leaving his braking to the very latest and getting into a slide. He held it, rammed the lever into first and headed for home, with Fangio unable to respond. Coming off the corner the Argentine could only wait, cursing, for his engine to build up revs. Indeed, on the long run down to the flag he was very nearly caught by Gonzales, whose drive had been inspired. Ascari, fourth, was four and a half seconds behind the winner. Quite close, all in all, after 507 kilometres (315 miles) of racing.

Monza 1953

It was due to be Ascari's last race for Ferrari. He had been World Champion in 1952, and was already assured of the 1953 title when they went to Monza for the final race of the year. He had won 11 of the last 13 Grands Prix, including seven on the trot at one point, records which will surely stand for ever. And now, when the season was concluded, he was leaving Ferrari, to the astonishment of the racing world, to drive for the new Formula 1 Lancia team. Therefore, he very much wanted victory in the Italian Grand Prix for the Commendatore, and it was assumed by all that he would get it.

Ascari, for all his Latin blood and obsessive superstitions, was very much a motor racing Bradman: phleg-

Plug change on de Graffenried's Maserati

matic, analytical, a ruthless winning machine. He was at his best in races (there were many) where he led from the start, left the opposition behind and simply reeled off the laps, lines inch-perfect, a model of precision. But he was far less at ease when he had to fight, perhaps because the situation rarely arose during much of his career. At Monza, in 1953, he had to fight.

Ascari was the fastest driver I ever saw, wrote Mike Hawthorn of his idol. *And when I say that, I include*

Fangio . . . Pole position became virtually Alberto's right during the early 1950s, and he duly set the best time at Monza, sharing the front row with Fangio's Maserati and Farina's Ferrari. On the second row were Marimon's Maserati and the Ferraris of Villoresi and Hawthorn.

From the start it was a four-car battle, with Ascari, Farina, Fangio and Marimon quickly breaking away from the pack. Two Ferraris and two Maseratis, all running perfectly.

Even by previous Monza standards, the 1953 race soon established itself as something out of the ordinary. For lap after lap the Italians fought the Argentines, the race order changing constantly, often several times within a single lap. The spectators were almost mesmerised, hardly believing that this could last until the flag.

Marimon finally broke the pattern soon after the halfway point when he spun at Vedano (later modified and renamed 'Parabolica'). The Maserati was lightly damaged. After a swift stop Onofre joined the group dicing for the lead, several laps down, but keen to help Fangio's bid to beat the Ferraris.

As this extraordinary race breathlessly developed, it became clear that no one was sand-bagging, that all were right at the limit. Fierce it may have been, but there was no lack of humour between Ascari and Fangio, who frequently grinned at each other as they hurtled, side by side, down to the next corner. Farina, by contrast, looked straight ahead at all times. For the icy Doctor, motor racing was never a frivolous matter . . .

Two laps to go. Obviously all would now be resolved in the last few yards of the race, and to add further to the spice of the moment the quartet was quickly coming up to lap some backmarkers. Fangio, Farina and Ascari crossed the line three abreast.

Into the last lap Ascari led, but there were no team orders at Ferrari in those days and he knew that Farina would try and beat him. Just behind them sat Fangio's Maserati and the blue and yellow car of Marimon. Ahead were a couple of tail-enders.

Approaching the last corner of the final lap Ascari knew that he had to go for it, hoping that the slower drivers had seen him. If he lifted off, the race was lost. Into Vedano he passed one car, then went inside the other. But he had overdone it slightly, and the Ferrari began to slide sideways. Farina, right behind, swerved to avoid his team-mate and got on the grass, while Fangio, canny as ever, somehow threaded through on the inside. Marimon attempted to follow his mentor, lost it and clouted Ascari's car.

The spectators, preparing themselves for a frantic scrabble to the line, looked on disbelievingly as Fangio's Maserati came alone into their sight. In the confusion the man with the flag forgot to wave it, and Juan Manuel, with a recovered Farina behind him, had to do another lap. A few minutes later Ascari and Marimon appeared, bloodied and without their cars . . .

Juan Manuel Fangio

Pau 1954

There were howls of dismay in France when, at the end of 1954, Jean Behra announced that he was going to Maserati for the following season. And this Gallic outrage was entirely unjustified, as the more sanguine of Behra's fellow countrymen realised. He had given three years of his life to Gordini, then the only French Grand Prix team, and had precious little to show for it. Better, he reasoned, for a French driver to be competitive in a red car than an also-ran in a blue one. Jean Behra was as intensely patriotic as any driver who ever lived, but saw no future in continuing with Amédée Gordini's under-financed, underpowered and unreliable cars.

Those three seasons had produced only two important victories for 'Jeannot'. In 1952, his first year as a Grand Prix driver, he had beaten the Ferraris to win the Reims Grand Prix, thereby establishing himself for all time as a national hero, his chequered helmet a symbol of hope and pride for a country in the motor racing wilderness. A fortnight earlier Pierre Levegh's gallant but foolhardy attempt to win Le Mans single-handed had failed at the last, handing victory to Mercedes-Benz. Behra's victory, therefore, could not have been more opportune.

Rumours persisted that Gordini may have had a helping hand from sympathetic officials that day in 1952, that Behra's car had a 2.5-litre engine beneath its bonnet – in a race for 2-litre cars. No matter. When David beats Goliath, history cares not what was in his sling.

The victory, alas, did not mark a turn in Gordini's fortunes. Despite Jeannot's fantastic spirit – he once drove his single-seater on public roads from Paris to Berne, the car being finished too late to make practice any other way – there were few finishes and many accidents.

The first major race of 1954 was the Pau Grand Prix, run under the new 2.5-litre Formula 1, and there were three-car teams from Ferrari, Maserati and Gordini. As expected, the Maranello trio of Farina, Trintignant and Gonzales led the way in practice, followed by the Maseratis of Marimon and Mieres and Behra's Gordini.

In the early laps of the race, however, the odds were evened when Farina was delayed with a serious misfire and then Gonzales retired with a blown engine. That left Trintignant in the lead, Behra second. The only French drivers of any consequence were one and two in a race in France: much was at stake.

At that time there was no set distance for the Pau Grand Prix, the race finishing at the end of the first lap after the three-hour mark. By the halfway point, Trintignant was 30 seconds clear of Behra, but then Jeannot began to close in. With a few minutes to go, the Gordini was right with the Ferrari, and the spectators screamed their support. Behra then calmly outbraked Trintignant and immediately pulled out a safe lead. The chequered flag fluttered down, and the little man came in to receive a rapturous welcome after a perfectly paced drive on one of the most exhausting circuits in the world.

The Gordini team took part in two further Pau Grands Prix before abandoning for good at the end of 1957. They had no success in them, both races being won by a Maserati – driven by Jean Behra . . .

Silverstone 1954

Grand Prix racing was in a state of shock in July 1954. When everyone assembled at Silverstone before practice for the British Grand Prix, the talk was only of Mercedes-Benz. Two weeks before, at Reims, the German team had returned after an absence of 15 years. They had entered three cars for the French Grand Prix, where Fangio and Kling had been first and second in both practice and race, and a third car, for Hans Herrmann, had set fastest lap. In terms of both pace and reliability, the streamlined W196 cars had everyone licked, and a similar showing was expected at Silverstone – particularly when Fangio put his car on pole position. On the front row with him were Gonzales (Ferrari), Hawthorn (Ferrari) and Moss (Maserati).

The grid, however, was somewhat misleading, for the presence of Fangio's silver machine at the front was the result of inspiration by the greatest driver of his time. In truth, the all-enveloping bodywork made the cars highly unsuitable for Silverstone, even the great Juan Manuel admitting that he found difficulty in judging the car's width when aiming for the apex.

That was a real problem at Silverstone. I believe that the open-wheeled cars, which were ready for the next race, would have been perfect for a small course. At Silverstone they marked out the course with oil barrels, I remember, and I kept hitting them because visibility from the cockpit was not good.

My car was very battered by the end . . .

Right at the back of the grid were the factory Maseratis, which had arrived too late for official practice. Their drivers were Ascari and Villoresi (on loan from Lancia, whose new D50 was still not ready to race) and the regular team leader, Onofre Marimon.

In wet and cold conditions Gonzales took the lead at the start. The Argentine was always brilliant at Silverstone, and this day he led comfortably from first to last. But Marimon's opening lap must stand as one of the greatest of all time. Thanks to missing practice he started in 28th position on the grid, yet he came by on

lap one in sixth place! This overshadowed even Ascari, who contrived to pass only 17 cars on that first lap! The great Alberto was to have a miserable race, blowing up his own car, then taking over Villoresi's 250F, which was to meet a similar fate a few laps later.

For a while Fangio held second place behind Gonzales, but the Mercedes was very definitely not in its element and began to drop back, falling into the clutches of Moss and Hawthorn, who had earlier put on a stirring duel for the huge crowd. Stirling seemed to have second place locked up, but the Maserati broke its rear axle after 80 of the 90 laps. His only con consolation was setting fastest lap – but that he had to share with no fewer than six others! Lap times were rounded off to the nearest second . . .

Gonzales finally won from Hawthorn by over a minute, with Marimon a superb third. Tragically, this was young Onofre's last race, for he was killed at the Nürburgring a fortnight later during practice for the German Grand Prix. This incident was to upset fellow-countryman Gonzales so much that he retired from Grand Prix racing at the end of the season.

Fangio, too, was much moved by Marimon's death, but managed to rise above it. At the Nürburgring, now in the open-wheel W196, he dominated, as he later did at Berne and Monza. The 1954 World Championship was his, and the following year Moss, who ran him close in Britain and Italy, was taken into the Mercedes team as his number two. Fangio remembers with affection and admiration his two years with the Three-Pointed Star.

Well, with Mercedes there was always peace of mind. I drove twelve Grands Prix for them, with eight wins, one second, one third, one fourth and one retirement. They were amazingly reliable, those cars. To win in 1954 and 1955 was easy because they were undoubtedly superior to every other car. They were quicker, and they lasted longer. But not at Silverstone!

1954 Vanwall Special

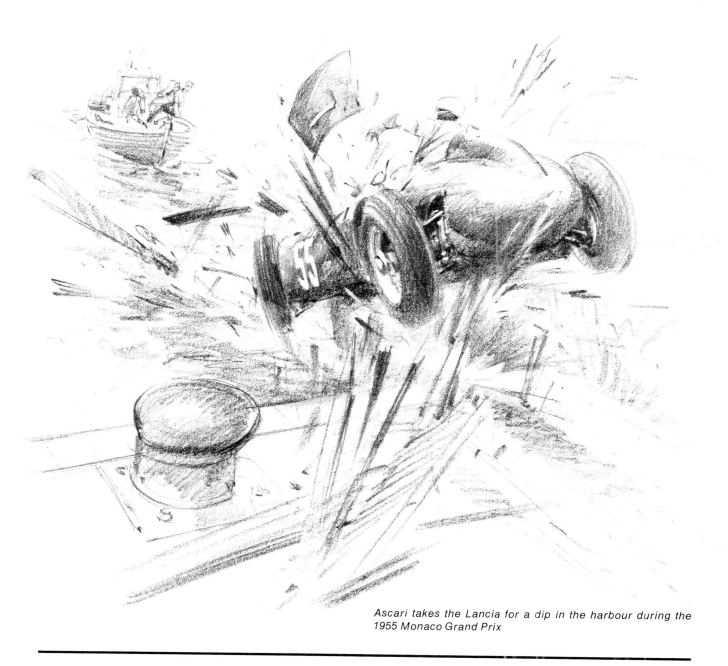

Ascari takes the Lancia for a dip in the harbour during the 1955 Monaco Grand Prix

Spa 1955

A lot of people feared for Eugenio Castellotti at Spa in 1955. Certainly he was a promising young driver, but even in normal circumstances he was considered more than fearless. And his circumstances at Spa were anything but normal.

He had joined the Lancia team as number two to Alberto Ascari, a man he revered. At Monte Carlo, the opening race of the European Grand Prix season, the two Italians provided the only possible threat to Mercedes-Benz, and when Fangio and Moss retired the victory should have gone to Ascari. But then Alberto had his famous accident at the chicane, the Lancia plunging through the straw bales and into the harbour. As Castellotti went on to finish second, his idol was taken off to hospital and later found to have nothing more than shock and a broken nose.

Only four days later Ascari was killed at Monza, in an accident which has never been satisfactorily explained. He had driven from his Milan home to the track simply to watch Castellotti testing a Ferrari sports

Castellotti and Farina at La Source hairpin, 1955 Belgian Grand Prix

car. On impulse he decided to put in a few laps himself, and, still in collar and tie and wearing his protegé's helmet, he crashed at Vialone, later renamed for him.

Italian motor racing was rocked by the tragedy, and a distraught Castellotti vowed that he would win the next race, at Spa, for the Maestro. At first Lancia intended to withdraw as a mark of respect to Ascari, but eventually Eugenio was allowed to enter a car privately. At the same time the story broke that Mike Hawthorn, dissatisfied with Vanwall, had been invited to replace Ascari. At Spa, the fastest circuit in Europe, Castellotti had much to prove, and the situation was potentially explosive. He did not know the circuit, he was in an over-emotional frame of mind, and he was on his own.

The first evening of practice he passed sensibly, learning about Spa, sorting out gear ratios. On Friday evening, though, Fangio and Moss became serious, recording the fastest times with their W196s, looking untouchable as they did so. But in the closing minutes of the session Castellotti, pumped up by adrenalin and patriotism and who knows what else, stormed round to beat Fangio by half a second. White-faced, he stepped from the cockpit of the dark red car, crossed himself and asked for a cigarette.

On Saturday it rained, so Eugenio's pole position was sure. For all that, he thundered round throughout the wet session, this time fractionally slower than Fangio. Each time a session finished and the harsh bark of the Lancia V8 was shut down people in the pits breathed a sigh of relief. But there was still the race . . .

Inevitably, perhaps, Castellotti could not stay with Fangio and Moss, although he led the rest of the pack. Behind him was another Italian, Farina, the haughty aristocrat of the old school, who thought that this young upstart needed a lesson in manners. Coming into La Source he overtook Eugenio on the inside – only to be repassed as the two cars left the corner. Farina did not appreciate this lack of respect and shook his fist, whereupon Castellotti squeezed the Ferrari over to the right, causing his senior rival to brush the toes of those in the pits . . .

At the end of the 15th lap Farina came by alone, but fears for Castellotti were allayed when news came through that he had pulled off at Malmédy with a broken gearbox. There was relief that his Belgian Grand Prix had ended undramatically, but sorrow that his tremendous effort had gone unrewarded. There had been something very moving about his homage to Ascari, but *bravura* alone was not enough to challenge Teutonic efficiency. Fangio and Moss ran unchallenged to the end.

Aintree 1955

Don't ask me if the Old Man let me win that day, because in all honesty I don't know. I can tell you that there were no pre-arranged tactics between us, no team orders from Neubauer. Perhaps it was suggested to Fangio that he should let me win, because it was the British Grand Prix. It's quite possible. But he wasn't the kind of guy who would ever have let me know it . . .

Perhaps that day at Aintree – July 16, 1955 – meant more to Stirling Moss than any other of his racing career. It presented him with his first victory in a Grand Prix, and it made him the first Englishman ever to win the British Grand Prix. Just a few weeks before he had won the Mille Miglia, only the second non-Italian to do so, but even that, he says, was not comparable with winning a Grand Prix before your own people.

In absolute terms, the 1955 British Grand Prix was not one of Stirling's legendary drives. From the first minute of practice it was obvious that a Mercedes was going to win. And two of their four drivers, Fangio and Moss, were clearly superior to the other pair, Kling and Taruffi. Led by Stirling, the German cars qualified 1-2-4-5, with only Jean Behra's Maserati able to upset the symmetry.

England's summer was unusually hot in 1955, and the day of July 16 was more torpid than most – another bonus for Moss and Fangio, who were fitter than most of their colleagues. Stirling led from the flag, but his Argentine master moved by him before the end of the first lap. This was the story of the 1955 Grand Prix season: Fangio leading, Moss on his tail. But at Aintree the pattern was broken, for the cars changed places on the third lap, Stirling then moving away to lead by as much as 12 seconds at one point.

No one could get near them. Behra kept his 250F in vague touch for 10 laps, but when he retired the only hint of a challenge to the Mercedes quartet was gone.

Kling and Taruffi were unable to match the pace of the leading pair, but they were beyond threat from any red or green interlopers.

As a race it was long and tedious, but for the spectators there was the excitement of an Englishman in the lead. Could Moss win? In the last third of the race Fangio speeded up, cutting back Stirling's lead. And Moss, ever the professional, obeyed 'slow' pit signals from Neubauer, although he did cut loose briefly towards the end, setting the fastest lap of the race in the process.

On the last lap the leading W196 was slowed right down, almost to a crawl, allowing the 'sister' car to close. Fangio, apparently on the limit, crossed the line only half a length behind.

Did the great man 'allow' his young team-mate to win that day? Moss was an Englishman in England, and

Fangio was never a selfish man. On only one other occasion was he ever 'beaten' by another Mercedes driver in a Formula I race; at Avus in the Berlin Grand Prix of 1954 he again finished a close second. It can have been no coincidence that the winner was Kling, a German on home ground. Mercedes, remember, did not go motor racing for sport. They returned in 1954 for cold-blooded business reasons: they wanted to revive flagging sales.

It is possible, then, that Moss was permitted to win at Aintree for political reasons. Beyond that, though, he seemed to have an edge over Fangio throughout the weekend, and most felt that victory was his right.

Today Fangio smiles when he remembers that day: *I don't think I could have won, even if I had wanted to. Moss was really pushing that day, and his car had a higher final drive than mine. It was quicker . . .*

Reims 1956

Peter Collins was very much the man in the news when he arrived at Reims late in June 1956. A month earlier he had won his first Grand Prix – at Spa, of all places – and suddenly people saw him as the man who just might bring the World Championship to Britain for the first time. It was not that Peter had cast off his light-hearted approach to life. On the contrary, he seemed that year to be more full of *joie de vivre* than ever. Nor had his talent changed. It was simply that now, as a member of the Ferrari team, his ability was translated into success.

At the French Grand Prix Collins was one of five Maranello entries, his team-mates being (in order of status) Fangio, Castellotti, de Portago and Gendebien. All drove the Lancia-based sidetank cars, which had excellent horsepower and a surfeit of understeer. At Reims, of course, cornering ability was of strictly secondary importance. On that score, the Commendatore's cars could not look at the factory Maserati 250Fs (whose drivers included Moss and Behra), but in a straight line the reverse was true. Hence, over a complete lap, Ferrari were in a race on their own.

Or were they? On the entry list also were three Vanwalls, for Schell, Hawthorn and Colin Chapman (yes, the very same). Earlier in the season, at the Silverstone International Trophy, Moss had won in one of the British cars, annihilating the Ferraris on the way.

However, this was a different race, a different day. At the fall of the flag the all-Ferrari front row moved away as one, with Fangio soon assuming his rightful place at the front. Quickly it appeared that the pattern was set, for the Maseratis could not keep pace, and Schell's Vanwall was out after only half a dozen laps.

It was not long, however, before Harry Schell was back in the game, for Mike Hawthorn, not at his best after taking part in the pre-GP 12-hour sports car race, was happy to hand over his car. Soon Schell was making fantastic progress and catching the Ferraris. By half-distance he was up with them.

Juan Manuel Fangio

This was an example of sheer animal courage and competitiveness, neither of which was lacking in the Franco–American. By no means the most gifted driver in the world, Schell could run with anyone at a track like Reims, and he revelled in the sensation of putting a dash of green in among the red.

It was hardly a fair contest, three against one, and the Ferrari drivers pulled every trick in the business to keep the Vanwall from the lead, chopping across Schell's bows, putting him on the grass, working together against a common enemy. Harry made it to second place at one stage, but eventually the car's fuel injection linkage began to break up, and that was the end of the challenge.

A couple of laps later, Fangio, too, was in the pits, losing nearly three minutes while a split fuel pipe was repaired. Now it was a straight fight between Castellotti and Collins, with the Italian narrowly in front. Soon Peter came by in the lead, at which point the two drivers were ordered to hold station, eventually crossing the line nose to tail. Ferrari had survived, but the Vanwall flare was in the sky . . .

Maseratis at the Nürburgring

Monaco 1956

Juan Manuel Fangio and Stirling Moss, the great Mercedes team-mates of 1955, were rivals once more the following year. Daimler Benz, domination complete, had withdrawn the Mercedes team from the sport, leaving their stars seeking employment. Logically, after trying the three British cars on offer at the time (BRM, Vanwall and Connaught), Moss returned to Maserati. And Fangio, for the first and only time in his career, opted for a season with Scuderia Ferrari. The 1956 season would give him his fourth World Championship, but it was one which gave him little pleasure. The great man's philosophy of life did not readily suit the politics of Maranello.

As well as that, Fangio did not enjoy the car Ferrari gave him to drive in 1956. When Lancia withdrew from Grand Prix racing, shortly after the death of Alberto Ascari, the company directors handed over their cars to Enzo Ferrari. And these, modified, wore the Prancing Horse throughout the 1956 season. The Lancia-Ferrari was a clumsy car, with pronounced

Moss leads Castellotti and Schell into Station hairpin at Monaco, 1956

understeer. Fangio, master of the elegant power slide, thrived on oversteer.

At Monte Carlo, the second Grand Prix of the year, he found the car particularly irksome. Power it had in plenty, but through the tight corners it could hardly get out of its own way. All Fangio's genius was required to put the car on pole position.

Next to him, in the middle of the front row, sat Moss and the Maserati 250F, half a second slower, twice as content. At some stage in their careers, all great drivers seem to develop a particular affinity for one car. Man and machine seem simply to belong together. With Stirling, it was the 250F.

No question about it. I don't know how many Grand Prix cars I drove, but the old 250F was my favourite. You know, I raced Maseratis in '54 and '56, and had the year with Mercedes in between. Now the Merc was definitely a better car, from pretty well every point of view, especially its reliability. But I always felt that it was an efficient machine, put together by efficient people. A means to an end. With Maserati, you were talking about a way of life, an emotional thing, and the 250F seemed to communicate that to you somehow. It's difficult to explain my feelings about it. At times you could curse it, when an oil pipe would break or something, costing you a race. But it was wonderfully satisfying to drive, because you always felt it was trying to work with you. Looking back on it, you could do anything with a 250F . . . and they were always such super looking cars, weren't they?

Moss took the lead at Monaco from the start, and he was still in first place at the end of the 100th, and last, lap. He remembers the race as being not particularly eventful. Behind him, however, the story was somewhat different.

Fangio is remembered for his fluency and ease of driving style, a brilliant man making a difficult art deceptively straightforward. But the Monaco Grand Prix of 1956 was a fugitive from the rest of his career. He drove that race as no other. On the second lap he went into Ste Devote too fast and spun, putting out Musso and Schell in the process. Rejoining in fifth place he quickly made up ground on those ahead, but at what cost to his car! Was it really the calculating brain of Fangio beneath the familiar brown helmet? The Lancia-Ferrari was travelling fast, but hitting kerbs everywhere, bouncing off straw bales and glancing walls. Shortly before half-distance he handed over what was left of the car to Castellotti, and rejoined in the Italian's fifth-placed *macchina*, well over a minute behind Moss. At the finish he was but six seconds adrift, setting yet another record on the final lap.

It was maybe the strongest race I ever drove. It was very difficult to overtake at Monaco, you know, even in those days! And I did overtake a few, I can tell you . . . Many people have said it was not Fangio in the car that day, but they don't know what was happening in the car! For me it was the fastest way around that circuit in that car. May not have been pretty to watch, but it was the quickest way . . .

For Moss it was a copybook race, without mistakes, and it gave him his first Grand Prix victory in a Maserati. In the final laps Fangio was reeling him in at a tremendous rate, but Stirling was paying out the line, assuming the master's role.

Nürburgring 1957

Even now, these many years later, I can feel fear when I think of that race. Only I knew what I had done, the chances I had taken. The Nürburgring, you know, was always my favourite circuit, without any doubt. I loved it, all of it, and I think that day I conquered it. On another day, it might have conquered me, who knows? But I believe that day that I took myself and my car to the limit – and perhaps a little bit more. I had never driven like that before, and knew I never would again . . .

Fangio's victory in the 1957 German Grand Prix stands for all time as part of racing legend undiminished by a surfeit of idolatrous prose. Only when the man himself looks back upon it, and admits that its recollection sends a shiver down his back, does it come back into focus as a staggering achievement. If we accept that Grand Prix racing has never known a greater talent, and that the race stands alone in his memory, then we must also accept that those at the Nürburgring bore witness to the summit of the racing driver's art.

The bare bones of the day are these: Fangio started from pole position with a time of 9 minutes 25.60 seconds, which was almost three seconds faster than Mike Hawthorn. Running on half-tanks, he took the lead on lap three and built up an advantage of half a

minute before pitting for fuel and tyres. The stop went badly, and he returned to the race almost 50 seconds adrift of the Ferraris of Hawthorn and Peter Collins. Ten laps remained.

For three laps Juan Manuel made no real impression on the two young Englishmen, but then, as he settled into his work, the World Champion began to close. In disbelief the timekeepers checked their watches: as a matter of routine now, Fangio was lapping 15 seconds under the old record, set the previous year – by himself, of course . . .

At the end of lap 19, the gap was 13 seconds. At the end of lap 20, the Maserati was right with the Ferraris! A new lap record was announced: 9 minutes 17.40 seconds. It was almost beyond belief. Fangio had beaten his own pole position time by more than eight seconds, and Hawthorn and Collins were done. Peter, now without a clutch, resigned himself to his fate.

This was the gentle Argentine at his most merciless. In a long, perfectly held, slide, the Maserati went by the first Ferrari, slipping one wheel off the road as it did so. Collins was peppered with small stones, one of which shattered his goggles. That left only Hawthorn, who fought back with everything he had. But Fangio was not to be denied, and took the flag almost four seconds ahead.

As he stepped from the car, the great man suddenly looked every minute of his 46 years. Only he knew . . . The victory, which clinched his fifth World Championship, was his last.

Aye, that Maserati . . . the 250F. Not very powerful, I recall, but beautifully balanced. A lovely car to drive. I felt I could do anything with it . . .

Monza 1957

No question about it, the Italians were nervous at Monza in 1957. Three weeks before the Grand Prix, Stirling Moss and Vanwall had completely outpaced the rest at Pescara, winning by three clear minutes. That was bad enough, but annihilation at Monza was unthinkable.

From the start of practice it was clear that only Maserati would be able to offer worthwhile opposition to the three green cars, for Ferrari's much-modified ex-Lancia V8 machines were coming to the end of their life, frankly off the pace at the high-speed *autodromo*.

Vanwall at Aintree in 1957

Jean Behra in a Maserati

*Fangio in a 250F Maserati being hounded by Luigi Musso in a
Lancia-Ferrari during the 1957 French Grand Prix at Rouen.
Fangio won, with Musso finishing second*

Italy's hopes, therefore, rested on Juan Manuel Fangio and Jean Behra, and for them Maserati brought along regular six-cylinder 250Fs and also the dramatically beautiful V12 car, which had appeared spasmodically through the season, but had been raced only once, by Carlos Menditeguy at Rouen. No one doubted its sheer horsepower at the top of the rev range, but it had very little lower down, which made life very difficult for the drivers. Monza, felt the Maserati engineers, would be one place where it could shine. During practice Fangio tried the car, but opted to stick with what he knew best. Behra eventually decided to race it.

Neither man, though, could live with the Vanwalls, and Moss looked certain to start from pole position. Right at the end of practice, however, the asthmatic, delicate, but hugely talented Stuart Lewis-Evans stormed round three-tenths faster than his team leader, and the issue was settled. With Tony Brooks third,

Tony Vandervell's cars had commandeered the front row, which did not sit well with the local populace. Overnight, therefore, the 3-2-3 grid suddenly became a 4-3-4 affair, with Fangio's red 250F joining the Vanwalls at the front!

The first 20 laps of the 1957 Italian Grand Prix will stand for all time as a supreme example of what motor racing can be, the three Vanwalls and two Maseratis leaving everyone else behind. It was an unforgettable battle. Three understeering Vanwalls with a decided advantage in straightline speed versus two oversteering Maseratis; the flat four-cylinder drone of the British cars against the mellow wail of the Maserati 'six' and the shriek of the V12. All five men led at some stage, but Fangio and Behra were clinging on, their cars not quite on level terms.

Such a pitch can never, it seems, be maintained. After 20 laps Brooks had to stop with a sticking

throttle, and then Lewis–Evans came in with a cracked cylinder head. Behra, constant wheelspin eating his tyres, fell back and eventually retired with an overheating V12 after a typically gallant display. It was now Moss against Fangio, but even the great Argentine had no real answer to the Vanwall. Stirling eventually went away, and towards the end of the 87-lap race looked as though he might actually lap the Maserati. At the flag he was 38 seconds ahead.

If Fangio was beaten that day, it was with honour. On pure horsepower he was outpaced, but he gave one of the greatest demonstrations of cold determination and Latin panache ever seen, time and again pitching the Maserati into sublime power slides in his efforts to keep on terms.

Tony Brooks: *I learned a great deal in that race. Monza was a wonderful place to race at that time, with none of these silly chicanes all over the place. Many of the corners were very, very quick, but not completely flat. The Curva Grande was especially nice. We'd approach at about 175 mph, I suppose, dab the brakes and go through at about 160.*

I thought I was taking this corner pretty quickly, and in the early stages I was dicing with Fangio for the lead. First time through Curva Grande, touch the brakes, turn in – and wham! he goes by on the inside, oversteering it on the throttle! Later in the lap I got by him again, and the next time through Curva Grande, wham! Exactly the same again. I don't know, maybe he wasn't braking at all . . .

The glory that day was to Moss and Vanwall, who had beaten the Italians before their own people. But Fangio, racing in Italy for the last time, showed his greatness at Monza for all to see.

Buenos Aires 1958

I suppose that, of all the Grands Prix I ever drove in, that was probably the one I least expected to win. Stirling Moss's victory at Buenos Aires in 1958 not only belongs in motor racing folklore but must rank as one of the most curious in Grand Prix racing history. Only ten cars took the start, and no one knew for sure that the event would count for the World Championship.

The confusion arose because of rule changes at the end of the 1957 season, the most far-reaching of which was a new regulation which stipulated the use of 'Avgas' aviation fuel rather than the 'dope' fuel of previous years. The Argentine organisers did not firmly announce their race until the middle of December, and its scheduled date – January 19 – left too little time for Vanwall and BRM to convert their engines for the new fuel. Jean Behra and Harry Schell, contracted to BRM for the season, found Maserati 250F rides, but, of the three-driver Vanwall team, only Moss was able to make alternative arrangements. Rob Walker offered him the use of his 2-litre Cooper-Climax, and Stirling accepted gratefully.

It's incredible, you know, says Stirling, looking back.

Alf Francis was the mechanic on that car, and Brabham had done a race with it towards the end of '57, running on the usual methanol mixture. In Argentine it still had a compression ratio to match, simply because there hadn't been time for Alf to do anything about it! I think he'd changed the carburettor jets, and that was about it . . .

For all that, the little blue and white car went well enough in practice, with Moss only a couple of seconds behind Fangio's pole position time, despite being about 100 brake horsepower down. The Cooper faced opposition from three factory Ferraris and six privately-entered Maseratis, and there was another problem, too. In the course of the first practice day, Stirling's wife inadvertently jabbed a finger into his eye! For the rest of practice he had to drive with a patch over it.

For the race, Moss's strategy was clear: he would try to go the distance on a single set of tyres. The Cooper had bolt-on wheels, and a tyre change would have taken for ever. After a careful start Stirling began to move through as, one by one, the leaders – Fangio, Behra, Hawthorn, Musso – made their stops. By three-quarter distance Moss led by a clear minute, but his

Stirling Moss

tyres were starting to wilt. Behind, and closing, was a confident Musso – confident because he felt sure that Stirling had to stop.

Throughout all this Moss was using all the guile at his command. As at the Nürburgring three years later, where he was also concerned about tyre wear, Stirling now positively sought out the slippery bits. Anything to conserve his tyres, which showed more and more canvas with every passing lap.

When Musso finally got the message, it was too late. Far from cruising easily, the Italian now really went to work, taking seconds from the Cooper with every passing lap. At the finish the Ferrari was less than three seconds behind. Another lap, and Musso would probably have been ahead. Stirling had judged it to perfection, and Cooper had won their first Grand Prix, as also had Rob Walker's team.

Luigi Musso never came so close to a Grand Prix victory again. An inveterate gambler, the Roman aristocrat was visited ('tis said), on the eve of the French Grand Prix by certain threatening characters who wanted their money. Prize money at the Reims race was by far the highest of the season. Perhaps that, combined with Musso's fanatical patriotism, spurred him into a fatal mistake as he chased Hawthorn through the flat out right-hander after the pits . . .

Monza 1958

For all the success that Stirling and I had with it, you know, the Vanwall was never what you would call a nice car to drive. Not really. It always had this tendency to understeer, for one thing, and the gearbox was one of the most diabolical things ever put together by man! I remember one race where I lost my clutch – Monaco, I think – and at the end my hand was like a piece of raw steak . . . Still, I mustn't complain too much about it. No one could deny that it got the job done.

By 1958 Tony Brooks had become worthy of inclusion among the great. Always superbly stylish, he applied great intelligence to the business of race driving, and, hallmark of the artist, made it seem effortless and straightforward. As season's end approached he had already won two classic Grands Prix, at Spa and the Nürburgring. For all that, though, his task at Monza was to help Stirling Moss to the title.

Mike Hawthorn was Stirling's rival in the World Championship, but Ferrari were in some turmoil,

shattered by the recent loss of Luigi Musso and Peter Collins. For the Italian Grand Prix Phil Hill and Olivier Gendebien were brought in to join Mike and Wolfgang von Trips.

Moss, Brooks and Hawthorn set the best times in practice, but when the race started Hill burst through from the second row and was in the lead as the field completed lap one.

I was nervous as hell before that race, Phil remembers. *I'd been driving Ferrari sports cars for years, and really gotten to the point where I thought they would never put me in a Grand Prix car. Finally the offer came – and it had to be at Monza! I just wanted the race to start so I could forget my nerves . . .*

The race began badly for Hawthorn, who overheated his clutch on the start line. Mike was in a low mental state at this time, having lost two team-mates in recent weeks, and in the course of the opening lap he witnessed an appalling accident between von Trips and Harry Schell, seeing the German flung from his Ferrari as it somersaulted into the trees at Lesmo. Although 'Taffy' suffered only a broken leg, Hawthorn could not envisage that he had survived.

For all that, he got on with the task in hand, and by lap five had passed Hill for the lead, soon to be joined by Moss. For several laps the two championship contenders fought an engaging duel, with the Vanwalls of Brooks and Stuart Lewis-Evans close behind.

Mike Hawthorn in the pits at Monza

46

The British team's challenge soon faded, however, Stirling retiring with a broken gearbox and Tony pitting to have an oil leak investigated. Hawthorn seemed set fair, but Brooks rejoined and really went to work. With 20 laps left he had climbed back to second place.

At this point Mike began to pay the penalty for hurting his clutch at the start. Increasingly it began to slip, and he was powerless to fend off the Vanwall. As the cars went into their last ten laps Tony passed the Ferrari right in front of the groaning stands.

So bad was Hawthorn's problem that he was caught by team-mate Hill on the last lap. Phil's race had been marred by a surfeit of tyre stops, but he continued to charge right to the end. In desperation Mike stuck out his arm and waved the American down. Fortunately Hill saw the signal and backed off – so much so that he almost stalled his engine! Half a minute behind Tony Brooks at the finish, Mike Hawthorn nevertheless got six points for second rather than four for third. And that was to decide the 1958 World Championship . . .

Casablanca 1958

This race, and the season which it climaxed, proved something for all time: the World Championship, in itself, is an absurdity. True, there have been years when the title mirrored the course of the season, when the World Champion was the man who won more races than the rest, but too often motor racing's crown has been put on the head of consistency, rather than competitiveness.

and set fastest lap (one), with Hawthorn finishing below second. And the farce of it was that Stirling went to the final round, at Casablanca, with three victories already scored, while Mike had only one!

There was a gap of six weeks between Monza and the Moroccan Grand Prix, an agonising wait for the two Englishmen, and during that time motor racing attracted an astonishing amount of publicity in their home

BRM mechanics at work

It was thus, to a startling degree, in 1958. After the Italian Grand Prix, with but one race to go, Mike Hawthorn led the Championship with 40 points, with Stirling Moss second on 32. With the scoring system as it was, to win the title Moss had to win (eight points)

country. Loyalties were split. Outside the sport, Moss had most people rooting for him. Already a national hero, he was driving a British car, previously having three times finished second to Fangio in the World Championship. Inside the business, Hawthorn was

Hawthorn followed by Bonnier (BRM), 1958 Moroccan GP

liked for his easy-going way of life and respected for his courage. As well as that, he was by now the only surviving member of Ferrari's original 1958 trio: Luigi Musso had been killed at Reims, and Mike was shattered by the fatal accident – right in front of him – of his close friend Peter Collins at the Nürburgring.

Numbers on the cars were not fixed for the season in those days, and when Hawthorn got to Casablanca, he was appalled to find that he had been allocated 2, the number used by both Musso and Collins at the time of their deaths. Mike quickly calmed down, however, when Olivier Gendebien, number 6 on the entry list, agreed to swap. His other team-mate at Casablanca was Phil Hill, who had made a stunning Ferrari F1 debut at Monza, and was happy to act as 'hare' in an attempt to break Moss's Vanwall.

Keeping to the script, Mike and Stirling duly took the first two places on the grid, joined on the front row by another Vanwall, that of Stuart Lewis-Evans. Next up were Jean Behra's BRM and the Ferrari of Hill.

There was, in the heat of Ain-Diab, a cold determination about Stirling Moss before the start. These were precisely the circumstances he most enjoyed; there was no question of tactics. He knew what he had to do: *It was great for me, really. Anything less than a win, and I'd lost the Championship. So the only thing to do was go for it, hope that my car would last and that Mike's wouldn't . . .*

Moss that day was at his unapproachable best, leading from the start and brushing off an early challenge from Hill. Third ran Tony Brooks' Vanwall, keeping Hawthorn back in fourth. Soon after half-distance, however, the Vanwall blew up, elevating Mike to third, which became second when Hill obeyed a pit signal to let his team leader through.

The race ran out that way, with Stirling a brilliant winner, nearly a minute and a half clear of Hawthorn, with Hill dutifully crossing the line immediately after Mike. To Moss also went the point for fastest lap, but the final championship tally was 42 to Mike, 41 to Stirling. Four victories had been beaten by one.

Until then, says Stirling, *winning the World Championship meant everything to me, but after that it lost meaning for me. I still wanted to win it, of course, but it didn't matter that much. And now, when I look back, I'm glad in a way that I didn't win it – not just once, anyway. Some pretty average drivers have won it once. I'd rather be remembered as the guy who should have won, and never did . . .*

In the pits after the race, Hawthorn celebrated, and then came the parties. But Mike had already made up his mind to retire. In the aftermath of Casablanca, his joy was diluted by the news that Lewis-Evans had been gravely burned in an accident shortly before the end. He died, back in England, a few days later. And three months after that Hawthorn himself perished in a road accident. He was only 29.

Reims 1959

It was a gorgeous car to drive, that Dino 246, says Tony Brooks, recalling his only season with Ferrari. *Of course, it was pretty well obsolete, being front-engined, because Cooper had pointed the way everyone had to go. It was heavy, yes, but it certainly had more horsepower than anything else, and at some circuits it was easy to win with it. The car was a bit like a Maserati 250F in that you could drive it on the throttle through the corners. And its gearbox! After two years with Vanwall, it was a revelation, believe me . . .*

The French Grand Prix of that year was one of those Brooks found 'easy to win.' Of all drivers in the sport's history, this man is perhaps the most underrated. Quiet and modest, he is nonetheless well aware of his own ability – as befits a man who was rarely overshadowed by Moss during their time in the Vanwall team together.

In many ways, that day at Reims was perfect for Brooks. The Dino 246 was in its element on the ultra-fast circuit, and Tony himself was always at his best on the quicker tracks. In practice he duly took pole position, followed by Brabham's Cooper and Phil Hill's Ferrari. On row two were Stirling Moss, abandoning his usual Rob Walker Cooper for a factory BRM (on loan to the British Racing Partnership), and the Ferrari of Jean Behra.

But that was practice, run in pleasant, summery weather. Race day was something else again, the hottest in Reims for many years. In the late morning the drivers were allowed a warm-up session – unheard of in those days – to check out the track surface, which was melting and breaking up. Clearly this was going to be a race of survival.

At the start, 'Toto' Roche did his usual trick, dropping the flag when no one, including himself, was ready. To avoid flattening the rotund geriatric, Behra braked hard, stalling his Ferrari. The crowd, rooting strongly for 'Jeannot,' howled its displeasure, and Behra probably regretted his charitable instincts.

Brooks, however, was gone, and even at this very early stage he seemed beyond challenge. Moss had the BRM up in second place at the end of lap one, followed by the Coopers of Masten Gregory and Brabham, but the Ferrari was out of their reach. After only nine laps Gregory, a man used to Kansas City summers, went into the pits, completely exhausted.

In the course of that long, sweltering afternoon, all the drivers suffered. In their desperation to get some air, Brabham and others smashed their windscreens, but this was a double-edged sword, for now they had less protection than ever from flying stones. Roy Salvadori and Graham Hill had to stop for replacement goggles because of it.

That race was sheer agony, from start to finish, Jack remembers. *The heat in the cockpit was just unreal, and you got showered with rocks and stuff every time you got behind another car. Towards the end I wasn't using the brakes at all – my feet were so badly burned that I couldn't put any pressure on the pedals . . .*

At Thillois Stirling spun the BRM, and was unable to restart it. Behra, charging through the field after his start line delay, over-revved the Ferrari and retired. When team manager Tavoni remonstrated with him, the Frenchman knocked him down. All round the circuit, cars weaved across the road, missed the apex, slid wide,

51

their drivers obviously nearing the end of their physical reserves.

All except for Brooks. This slightly-built man from the North of England had truly astonishing stamina. In 50 laps he made not the tiniest error, drove faster and more neatly than anyone. While all around him collapsed, Tony gratefully accepted a bottle of water, drank from it, climbed onto the rostrum and waved contentedly to the crowds. Perfectly straightforward, this business of winning Grands Prix . . .

Phil Hill in a Ferrari spins in front of Moss in a BRM, 1959 French Grand Prix

Sebring 1959

After the Italian Grand Prix of 1959 three men remained in contention for the World Championship. Stirling Moss, Tony Brooks and Jack Brabham then faced a wait of three clear months before settling the issue in, of all places, Florida. Formula 1 went to Sebring in 1959, for the very first American Grand Prix.

All three were familiar with the airfield circuit, of course, having raced there in the traditional 12-hour sports car race, and, remarkably, they set the fastest times in practice and should have made up the front row.

Stirling, predictably, took pole position with Rob Walker's Cooper-Climax, three whole seconds quicker than Jack's factory car, with Tony's front-engined Ferrari Dino 246 next up. After a protest by Harry Schell, however, an improved time was 'discovered' for the Franco-American, and his privately-entered Cooper was moved onto the front row, Brooks being demoted. There has always been some doubt that Schell's car covered the entire 8.4-kilometre (5.2-mile) circuit on its quickest lap . . .

All in all, the field for the first US Grand Prix was a curious one, with Moss's Cooper at one end and

Rodger Ward's USAC Midget dirt car – 44 seconds slower! – at the other.

The pantomime involving Schell may well have had a significant effect on the outcome of the World Championship, for Brooks, now on the second row of the grid, had Ferrari team-mate Wolfgang von Trips right behind him, and during the course of the first lap the German inadvertently clouted the back of Tony's car. As Moss and Brabham, first and second, came by at the end of the opening lap, Brooks brought the Ferrari in for a quick check over. With the World Championship at stake, it seemed an astonishing decision. Tony's explanation is fascinating.

Taffy clouted my rear wheel, and I decided to stop. Now, at an earlier stage of my career I wouldn't have done, and even then my natural inclination was to press on. Believe me when

I say that that would have been the easiest thing to do. But I made myself come in and have the car checked over.

My whole racing philosophy changed somewhat after I flipped a BRM at Silverstone in 1956 – and completely when I did the same thing with an Aston Martin at Le Mans the year after. Each shunt was caused by a problem with the car, and I made a firm mental decision never to try to compensate for a car's mechanical deficiencies. If something wasn't working properly, too bad. I always felt it was morally wrong to take unnecessary risks with one's life because I believe that life is a gift from God, and that suicide is morally unacceptable. To me, driving a racing car which may be unsound or damaged is not exactly suicide, but it's verging towards it.

I felt a moral responsibility to take reasonable care of my life, and I think this change of philosophy may have cost the

McLaren and Trintignant in the 1959 American Grand Prix

title in '59. I lost half a lap on the pit stop, and still finished third. In my own mind, though, I'm sure I did the right thing . . .

One corner of the Championship triangle, then, was out of it virtually from the start, and on the fifth lap Moss retired from a dominant lead with broken transmission, leaving Brabham home free. The Australian, with team-mate Bruce McLaren close behind, ran easily at the front of the field, with Cliff Allison's Ferrari third. In the late stages of the race, however, there was a terrific charge by Maurice Trintignant, the French veteran bringing his Walker Cooper ever closer to the works cars.

On last lap, Brabham ran out of fuel, leaving the youthful McLaren to hold off Trintignant alone. At the flag Bruce was but half a second ahead, cool and unflustered for his first Grand Prix victory. Trintignant crossed the line, then Brooks. And finally Brabham arrived, completely exhausted, having pushed his car almost a mile to the finish. Not ideal circumstances in which to clinch a World Championship, but better, as Jack said, than losing . . .

Graham Hill in a BRM spins off at Copse Corner at Silverstone, ending his epic drive in the 1960 British GP

Oporto 1960

The Grand Prix circus went to Portugal for the third, and last, time in 1960, returning to the street circuit in Oporto which had been used two years previously. The 7.4-kilometre (4.6-mile) track abounded in what were called 'natural hazards' at the time, these including kerbs, lamp posts and even tramlines . . .

In August 1960 Jack Brabham came to the end of a very hot streak. He had won the last four Grands Prix on the calendar, at Zandvoort, Spa, Reims and Silverstone, and his second consecutive World Championship was as good as won. The Australian's luck, his rivals fervently maintained, had to change.

In Portugal the grid was a curious one. Brabham, as usual was on the front row, but his company there was unexpected. On pole position was John Surtees, who had finally abandoned his MV Agustas and was concentrating on cars, driving a works Lotus in only his third Grand Prix. And next to him, blossoming briefly during a disapponting season with BRM, was Dan Gurney. Stirling Moss, returning to Formula 1 only a couple of months after his disastrous accident at Spa, was fourth fastest with Rob Walker's Lotus.

In the heat of the afternoon Gurney snatched the lead at the start, with Brabham and Moss behind. On lap two, though, Brabham's Cooper momentarily appeared to have a mind of its own . . .

That was the most incredible thing. I moved to the inside to try and take Stirling – and suddenly I had no steering! It was as if someone had grabbed the wheel out of my hands . . .

Like the famous sequence in the film *Genevieve,* the Cooper had got stuck in the tramlines! Temporarily helpless, Brabham weaved across the road – between two cars – and emerged from the corner on a very curious line. Eventually he managed to disentangle himself and set off once more, not knowing whether to laugh or cry. By now he was back in eighth place.

Gurney led decisively for the first ten laps, but the BRM was beginning to lose oil, which was blowing onto the rear tyres, and a spin dropped him way down the field, allowing Surtees to take command.

Colin Chapman's hopes rested entirely on John, for Jim Clark, his car hastily and none too prettily repaired after a practice accident, was out of the picture. And Moss was in and out of the pits with a misfire on the Walker car.

Behind Surtees was a tremendous battle between Brabham and the front-engined Ferrari of Phil Hill, the American keeping his obsolete car in contention by sheer inspiration and courage. Eventually Phil hit some straw bales, and Jack was left with a secure second place, albeit out of touch with the leader.

More than brilliance is needed to win World Championships, however, as history has frequently shown. You need consistency and you need luck. On lap 37, with 18 remaining, Brabham inherited the lead. Since the start of the race a leaky tank had allowed fuel to seep onto Surtees's shoes. When John put the brakes on, his foot slipped off the pedal and jabbed the throttle. In an instant the Lotus was into the bales, its radiator split. And Brabham cantered in for his fifth win on the trot.

Monza 1960

There was a great hue and cry in April 1982 when the majority of the British teams decided to boycott a Grand Prix in Italy, presumably in the hope that without them the race would be a disaster. If that was their motive, a glance at the history books would have told them that their gesture was an empty one. The Brits boycotted Imola in 1982, just as they had given Monza a miss in 1960. In neither case was their absence significant. For a successful race in Italy, you need Ferrari. Nothing else.

The British teams stayed away from Imola because they were sulking. They had found a loophole in the regulations, exploited it, and now found the loophole plugged. They were out, so, for the San Marino Grand Prix, they were taking their bat and ball home.

In 1960 they were sulking because of the Monza organisers' decision to use the combined banking/road circuit for the 31st Italian Grand Prix. This accent on all-out speed, said the Brits, would favour the outdated, front-engined Ferraris, which had more power than

anything else, but were obsolete in terms of road-holding. This was a remarkably perspicacious observation . . .

To the Italians it mattered little. Enzo Ferrari entered four cars, one of them the new rear-engined Formula 2 car, which had recently triumphed in its debut race at Solitude. This, after all, was the basis of the 1961 Formula 1 car, and the Commendatore was keen to put race miles on it. The British teams, it should be remembered, had still not accepted, in September 1960, that a new Formula 1 was being introduced for 1961. *Plus ça change . . .*

Just as FOCA would discover 22 years later, the Italians turned out in their usual vast numbers to watch the Grand Prix. The red cars were there, with Phil Hill on pole position, followed by Richie Ginther and Willy Mairesse. Sixth fastest overall was Wolfgang von Trips in the Formula 2 car. A total of 16 cars were on the grid, seven of them F2 machines.

The race was, of course, a mere formality for Ferrari,

with Hill and Ginther taking turns in the lead, Mairesse running a consistent third, and von Trips having the measure of all the Formula 1 opposition, save Giulio Cabianca's Ferrari-engined Cooper. The plan was obviously for Hill to win, he being the number one driver, and this the great American duly did. It was Phil's first Grand Prix victory. A year later he would repeat it, at the same time clinching the 1961 World Championship. Ferrari, ready as usual for changes in F1 rules, dominated the season.

In 1961 the Italian Grand Prix was again run on the combined banking/road circuit, and the British teams had put away all their previous qualms, including those of safety, and were back. No fewer than 32 cars took the start, all of them rear-engined. Hill's 1960 victory was the last ever by a front-engined car.

Phil Hill, Von Trips, Ginther and Mairesse on the banked section in the 1960 Italian Grand Prix

Monaco 1961

Was Stirling the best of his time? Oh yes – and by a long way. Fortunately for the rest of us, though, he usually compromised himself by not running for a factory team. If he had, he would have been World Champion who knows how many times. And even without works back-up he still had days when you just couldn't beat him. Monaco '61 was one of those . . .

Richie Ginther remembers the race fondly, for he

emerged from it with almost as much credit as did
Moss, who won. It was, by any standards, a remarkable
event.

Stirling had won the previous year's Monaco Grand
Prix in fairly straightforward fashion, driving Rob
Walker's Lotus 18. At the time the car was new, a
replica of the factory Lotus cars, in the final season of
the 2.5-litre formula, but by May 1961 the new 1.5-litre
Formula 1 had come into play, and Ferrari – as ever
more ready than the rest – looked set to dominate.
Their new V6 engines gave as much as 30 horsepower
more than the old four-cylinder Coventry Climax, one
of which was in Moss's car, again entered by Rob
Walker's team, and again a Lotus 18, rather than the
latest 21.

The results of the practice were that Stirling took
pole position, with 1 minute 39.1 seconds, followed by
Ginther's lovely sharknose Ferrari and Jimmy Clark's
factory Lotus. Behind were two more Ferraris, of Phil
Hill and Wolfgang von Trips.

Ginther, in only the fourth Grand Prix of his life,
really made a name for himself at Monaco. In a year at
Maranello he had established himself as a superlative
test driver, and during the winter had done the bulk of
the development work. For this opening race of the
season, therefore, he was assigned the only Ferrari with
the newest 120 degree engine, and he certainly made the
most of it, taking the lead at the start and edging away
to head the field easily after half a dozen laps. Ten laps
later, though, he had been passed by both Moss and Jo
Bonnier (Porsche). Shortly afterwards team-mate Hill,
too, was by him.

When Bonnier retired, it was Moss versus the
Ferraris, a mesmeric battle between driving genius and
horsepower. For 50 laps the red cars kept up the pursuit,
Stirling never leading by more than 10 seconds. Then,
as the race entered its final quarter, Ginther got his
second wind, passed Hill and really set about the Lotus.

The tension of those final laps was extraordinary.
You heard the flat drone of the Climax and then the
howl of the Ferrari, and you knew that Ginther must
win. Then you watched the perfect timing of a Moss
lapping manoeuvre, complete with wave of thanks,
and you felt that all was under control. At the flag
Stirling was 3.6 seconds to the good.

An examination of the facts puts that race into
perspective. Both Moss and Ginther ran the entire 100
laps at an average speed equal to their best qualifying
laps, and their shared fastest lap was three seconds
quicker than they had managed during practice.

MICHAEL TURNER '61

Stirling was to describe it as 'perhaps my greatest race.' Richie has no doubts.

That was definitely the best drive of my life. You know, that race was long in those days, going on three hours. I was right on the limit all the way, and I think Stirling was, too.

Unbelievable, really, when I think back to it. That son-of-a-gun . . . you know, in the Monaco programme they credit me with the lap record that year – but he equalled it the lap after I did it! Hey, any time you did well against him, you knew you'd really done something . . .

Zandvoort 1961

The 1961 Dutch Grand Prix took place just eight days after Stirling Moss's fabled victory at Monte Carlo. In the Principality Stirling's genius, allied to the roadholding of Chapman's Lotus 18, had been enough to see off the horsepower of Maranello, and there was a brief period of euphoria in British motor racing.

In Holland, though, the extent of the Ferrari menace became clear. After practice the front row was all red –

Phil Hill, Wolfgang von Trips, Richie Ginther. Moss was next up, sharing the second row with the BRM of Graham Hill. Far back – 11th of the 15 starters – was Jimmy Clark, leading the Lotus factory team on this occasion, for Innes Ireland had been hurt at Monte Carlo.

The race was effectively settled on the first lap, von Trips rocketing away from the line into a lead he never

Ferraris in the pits at Nürburgring, 1961

Von Trips and Phil Hill chase through the sand dunes at Zandvoort

lost. After a single lap he led by two clear seconds, with Graham Hill second, Phil Hill third. It was, however, the fourth man who brought gasps from the crowd, for Clark had passed seven cars during the course of lap one!

There lay the story of the day. For most of the race Jimmy battled with Hill's Ferrari for second place, leading it for a long way. It was the classic confrontation: handling versus horsepower. Every time around the beautiful red shark-nosed car would howl past the pits, pulling clear of the green cigar down Zandvoort's long main straight. And through the twisty sand dunes of the rest of the lap, Clark would claw it all back.

Eventually the Ferrari began to pull away. As the Lotus's fuel load lightened, its handling advantage diminished, and Clark settled back for an honourable third place, having set a new lap record which bettered the Ferraris' pole position time.

Serenely ahead of all this was the elegant von Trips, who duly came in for his first Grand Prix victory. Another, equally dominant victory followed in the

rains of Aintree two months later. When 'Taffy' went to Monza in September, he led the World Championship, team-mate Hill his only rival for the title. After taking the pole, the Count made a poor start, touched wheels with Clark on lap two, and died as his Ferrari vaulted off the road. Several spectators were also killed, bringing from the Vatican a strong suggestion that motor racing should be banned.

The handsome von Trips knew nothing whatever of racing cars, save how to drive them. And that was his passion. Through most of his career he was known more for crashing than winning, but during his final season he drove beautifully, a man at last fulfilled. Zandvoort was the beginning of what should have been the German's World Championship, a day in the sun when he drove flawlessly.

Only 15 cars started that day in Holland, a number laughable by the all-singing razzmatazz standards of today. But the race is unique in the sport's history, and will inevitably remain so. All 15 finished – and not one made so much as a pit stop . . .

The drivers Trintignant and Ginther were eliminated from this first-corner accident at Monaco, 1962, while Ireland (34) span but continued the race

Rouen 1962

As a race, the 1962 French Grand Prix was unremarkable. But it is remembered for two reasons: first, it provided Porsche with the only Grand Prix victory achieved by the German company during a brief two-year dalliance with Grand Prix racing; second, it was the only race of Jimmy Clark's magnificent career in which the great Scotsman was very obviously – and self-admittedly – off form.

At that time, motor racing was in search of a leader.

Three months earlier, at the Easter Monday Goodwood meeting, Stirling Moss had been severely injured in an accident which remains without explanation. For so many years he had been indisputably the 'Best', and now he was gone from the scene. Several aspired to his position, but it was obvious that only Clark could lay reasonable claim. In the early and mid-1960s, a quartet emerged, comprising Jimmy, John Surtees, Dan Gurney and Graham Hill. Membership was acquired by a

variety of means, from the genius of Clark to the hard graft of Hill. At a given race you could assume that, all things being equal, Jimmy would win and the remaining trio would figure.

At Rouen, a true driver's circuit, Clark inevitably took pole position with the Lotus 25, with Hill's BRM second, Surtees's Lola fifth, Gurney's Porsche sixth. But if practice followed a predictable pattern, the race did not, with Hill taking the lead at the start, chased by Surtees, Clark and Gurney. *I have to say,* recalled Jimmy later, *that I was just plain off form at Rouen that day. I can't explain it. Physically, I felt fine, but nothing seemed easy and straightforward. It was the only day I can remember when I simply didn't feel like going motor racing . . .*

Graham Hill, by contrast, was at his best, only Surtees able to keep the BRM in sight. And when John stopped at quarter-distance with a misfiring engine, the race appeared to be over, Hill now leading Clark by more than 15 seconds. But soon after the halfway mark Graham was rammed by Jack Lewis's brakeless Cooper and the BRM spun, letting Jimmy into the lead for the first time.

The Lotus was in front for only four laps before Clark retired at the pits with broken front suspension. And now Hill led once more, by almost half a minute, but the BRM eventually came to a halt with fuel injection problems, and the race was left to Gurney. He was required only to cruise the last 12 laps to win his

Gurney, Taylor (Lotus) and Trintignant (Lotus), French Grand Prix 1962

first Grand Prix.

A few weeks later Daniel Sexton took the flat-eight Porsche to another victory, in the Solitude Grand Prix, but Rouen was to stand as the team's only World Championship triumph. At the end of the 1962 season they decided to return to what they knew best: sports car racing. Gurney, meanwhile, went off to join Jack Brabham in the Australian's own team, but he did not win again until the middle of 1964 – in the French Grand Prix at Rouen . . .

Nürburgring 1962

The 1961 German Grand Prix stands as one of the most exciting in the history of the sport. As at Monaco that year, it was Stirling Moss against the Ferraris, and, as at Monaco, Stirling beat them fair and square.

At the Nürburgring the following year there was another fantastic tussle for victory, but this time the trio was different. In 1961 the protagonists had been Moss, Phil Hill and Wolfgang von Trips. Now, in August 1962, von Trips was dead and Moss was convalescing

and the BRM went over it, the oil tank splitting as it did so. Instantly oil spewed onto the rear tyres, and the car went out of control, spinning into a ditch and destroying itself. Graham was completely unhurt, and it says much for his composure that he later took out the spare BRM

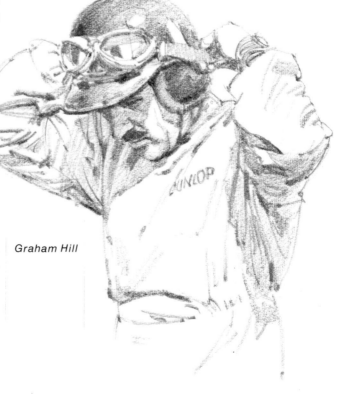

Graham Hill

after his Goodwood accident which ended his Grand Prix career. Hill was back again, once more in a shark-nose Ferrari, but the Italians had fallen on hard times, their cars uncompetitive, their team wracked by internal disputes. How much can change in a year!

After Stirling's unhappy departure, Jimmy Clark quickly asserted himself as the natural pacesetter, but Graham Hill, Surtees and Gurney were worthy rivals. It was fitting, therefore, that at the Nürburgring these four, each driving a different make of car, should make up the front row, with Dan's Porsche on pole position.

Practice was not without incident. On the Friday afternoon Hill was rushing down the steep and very fast Fuchsrohre when he spotted something lying in the road. At that speed there was no question of swerving,

Graham Hill chased by Surtees (Lola) and Gurney, 1962 German Grand Prix

Graham Hill chased by Surtees (Lola) and Gurney, 1962 German Grand Prix

and qualified second.

What did he hit? A television camera, dropped from Carel de Beaufort's Porsche a few seconds earlier. And as Hill stepped from the wreckage he saw Tony Magg's Cooper hit the BRM's oil. That car, too, was written off, although the South African escaped.

The four leading drivers not only started 1-2-3-4, but finished in those places as well. Clark took no part in the lead battle for he forgot to turn on his fuel pumps on the line and stalled as the flag fell. Soon he was on his way and driving just a little too fast for the wet conditions. After one or two mammoth slides he wisely reconsidered and settled for fourth place.

Hill, Surtees and Gurney circulated together for well over two and a half hours, their driving faultless, cars running perfectly. Little more than four seconds covered them as they crossed the line. It was, Graham later said, the most mentally taxing race of his life.

Trevor Taylor

Spa 1963

The true greatness of Jimmy Clark was never more convincingly seen than at Spa, partly because it was the circuit which, above all others, taxed every quality the racing driver should possess. That being the case, it was inevitable that a man of Clark's talent would shine there. What made his Spa performances exceptional was the fact that they were achieved in spite of his intense dislike of the place.

Jimmy's first Belgian Grand Prix was the tragic event in 1960, his opening season with Lotus. In practice, the Lotuses of Stirling Moss and Michael Taylor crashed disastrously after mechanical failures, and in the race one of Clark's team-mates, Alan Stacey, was killed. A few minutes before that the abnormally brave young Chris Bristow also lost his life, flung from his car after making a mistake at the ultra-fast Burnenville. This happened right in front of Clark, and made a very deep

impression on him. For ever after, he associated Spa with tragedy.

For all that, he won there on four consecutive occasions, beginning in 1962. The following year there was heavy rain at the start . . .

Jimmy's getaway was sensational. After two troubled days of practice he started only from the middle of the third row, yet through the first corner his Lotus was in front, followed by Graham Hill's BRM, which had taken pole position. As the field disappeared up the hill in a wall of spray the two leaders were already 100 yards clear.

A hush settled over the grandstand a few minutes later. Quite obviously there had been a major accident somewhere. Clark had been through, with Hill a couple of seconds behind, then . . . nothing. And then there was a quite audible sigh of relief as Brabham came

Clark and de Beaufort (Porsche), 1963 Belgian GP

Jim Clark

through, then Gurney, Mairesse, McLaren and the rest. Jimmy and Graham were 15 seconds ahead!

For three laps Hill did not lose anything to Clark, but thereafter the Lotus went inexorably away. The BRM was out with gearbox trouble soon after half-distance, and Jimmy eventually won by almost five minutes from McLaren. It was a stupefying demonstration. In the last few laps, when the rain reached monsoon proportions he was lapping at under 130 kmh (80 mph), having recorded over 216 kmh (134 mph) in practice!

Clark's drive apart, the 1963 Belgian Grand Prix was notable for the debut of 19-year-old Chris Amon, who made an excellent impression, climbing to seventh place in the early stages before his engine blew up. A soothsayer could have done Chris a favour that week-end by telling him that over the next 13 years he would drive in 95 further Grands Prix with no improvement in his luck . . .

There was humour, too, at Spa that year, for the ATS cars made their first appearance. Moreover, they took everyone by surprise, literally and metaphorically. The shambolic Italian outfit arrived late and set up shop away from the paddock, installing themselves at Malmédy. When Phil Hill came by the pits on his first lap there was general astonishment, for no one knew of the team's arrival! Later, when they looked at the appalling 'engineering' on the cars and noted that the engines were actually imprisoned in the chassis (removal required the use of a hacksaw!), they ceased to be amazed . . .

Jo Bonnier

Monaco 1964

That Jimmy Clark never won the Monaco Grand Prix is one of those twists of motor racing fate. The legendary Scotsman triumphed in every other Grand Prix on the calendar at some stage during his career, but in the Principality the numbers never came up for him.

Nor was it due in any way to weakness on his part. If Monte Carlo requires a special technique, then Jimmy had it. He drove in the Monaco Grand Prix six times, and started four of them from pole position. But never once was he running at the end.

Such is the way of it. Graham Hill won the race five times, but never took the British, which he wanted more than any other – and which Clark won on five occasions!

In 1964 Jimmy and the Lotus 25 duly set the best practice time at Monaco, followed by Brabham, Hill, Surtees and Gurney. They faced 100 laps on a very hot afternoon, but Clark went away as if in a sprint race. Out of the tunnel for the first time the Lotus led, astonishingly, by 200 yards, but at the chicane Jimmy made one of his scarce mistakes and left his braking too late. Somehow he made it through the left-right flick, but on the harbour front his nearside rear wheel clipped the straw bales.

Clark being Clark, the Lotus did not spin as it bounced across the road, but the anti-roll bar mounting was cracked by the impact, and one side was trailing in the road, setting up a welter of sparks. For all that, he led comfortably from Brabham, Hill and Gurney, but for how long?

Natural genius compensated for the Lotus's now unpredictable handling and Jimmy pulled out a sizeable lead, but officials were concerned about the trailing roll-bar and contemplated putting out the black flag. Before they could do so, Colin Chapman brought his man in, ripped away the debris and sent him back into the race. He was now third behind Dan Gurney and Graham Hill.

The second half of the race looked sensational in prospect, with the three leading runners in a tight bunch. On lap 53 Graham set a new lap record (which was to stand for the rest of the day) and took the BRM into the lead for the first time, immediately pulling slightly clear of Gurney and Clark. Dan's Brabham retired shortly after with a broken gearbox, whereupon Jimmy tried unsuccessfully to claw back to the leading BRM.

In the dying laps of the race the Lotus began to misfire, Clark finally pulling off on the hill to Casino Square with four laps to go. He was classified fourth.

For Hill it was a typical Monaco triumph, pacey yet unflustered. In the end he won by a clear lap from team-mate Richie Ginther, whose race represented a saga of pure courage. Just a month before the little American had somersaulted his BRM at Aintree. He went to the grid at Monte Carlo with ribs strapped up, a mass of semi-healed cuts and bruises, and he finished the race with the palm of one hand completely skinned. The BRM's gear lever knob had come away in the early laps.

Zandvoort 1964

After 1961, when Ferrari domination was challenged only by the brilliance of Moss, the years of the 1.5-litre Formula 1 conformed to a pattern. Stirling was gone from the scene, but Jimmy Clark quickly assumed his role as the natural pacemaker. Once in a while Gurney or Hill or Surtees would have a weekend of superiority, but usually Clark had a considerable edge. There was a total of 39 races during the last four years of the formula: Jimmy won 19, Graham 10, Dan and John three apiece. And during those years only four other drivers tasted victory, none of them more than once.

If it was a normal weekend, then, Clark would win, and it was that way at Zandvoort in 1964. On this occasion, however, he did not take pole position, that going to Gurney's Brabham. Third was Hill, fourth Surtees. Four drivers, four different cars. A quartet

warming up, asserting itself as usual.

Jimmy, though, was ever the soloist, and on a hot afternoon he took the Lotus straight into the lead, where it remained throughout. It was a Clark set piece, reeled off without apparent effort. In the early laps Gurney, Hill and Surtees held station behind him, but the gap widened inexorably. Big John moved the Ferrari up to second by quarter-distance, and then Dan had his usual luck. The American stopped to report a vagueness in the car's steering. Almost unbelievably, one of the steering wheel's spokes had sheered, and the Brabham team did not have a replacement . . .

Hill, too, was in trouble, the BRM V8 suffering from fuel vapourisation. For many laps his neck muscles underwent torture as the car made its irregular progress round Zandvoort, but eventually he came in. Cold

water was sloshed over the fuel pump, and temporarily the problem was solved. At the end, Graham was well pleased with fourth place.

By the time Clark finally acknowledged the chequered flag, many spectators were dozing quietly in the heat. At no stage had he been threatened, and his victory margin over Surtees was almost a full minute. Third, as he had been at Monte Carlo a couple of weeks earlier, was the Lotus number two, Peter Arundell. In this, his first Formula 1 season, Arundell looked very definitely like a future star, but his career was effectively, and tragically, ended in a dreadful accident in the Reims Formula 2 race a few weeks later. He returned to Lotus in 1966, but he was not the same driver.

The first World Championship points of Chris Amon's long career came in this race, the New Zealander taking fifth place in the Parnell Lotus-BRM (which showed unaccustomed reliability on this occasion!), ahead of privateer Bob Anderson and the Coopers of Bruce McLaren and Phil Hill. Fastest lap went – of course – to Clark, who set his best time as early as lap six, while working through his normal procedure of demoralising the rest.

It seemed like an endless race, recalled Clark later. For some reason I'd been playing around with the strap on my goggles just before the start, and when I put them on they were far too tight. There was no time to adjust them, and they really dug into my face. After only a few laps I had the worst headache I can ever remember – to the point that I almost wished the engine would break or something! All I wanted to do was lie down and close my eyes . . .

Mexico 1964

Graham Hill's BRM won the 1964 American Grand Prix at Watkins Glen, with John Surtees' Ferrari second. As usual, Jimmy Clark dominated with the Lotus 25, but the Scot retired at half-distance. And that result meant that all three were in contention for the World Championship, with Hill a heavy favourite. He had already scored in six races, and could add to his total of 39 points only by finishing third or better. Surtees had 34 points from five races, and Clark 30 from four. Jimmy, therefore, needed to win in Mexico, the last round.

After practice Clark was on the front row (pole position, as usual!), Surtees on the second and Hill on the third. Once again John opted for the V8-engined Ferrari, having more faith in its reliability than the demonstrably quicker flat-12 car which was assigned to Lorenzo Bandini. The Italian deeply admired Surtees, and promised before the race to do all he could to help him to the title. That he was certainly to do . . .

As at Watkins Glen three weeks earlier, the Ferraris were entered by the North American Racing Team and painted in the national racing colours of the USA. This was one of Enzo Ferrari's occasional theatrical gestures, a protest against the Italian Automobile Club and the FIA for their refusal to homologate the LM racing coupés as GT cars. The Commendatore was also mumbling that he would never allow his cars to race in Italy again. And nor did he – until the next race in Italy.

The Mexican Grand Prix began badly for Graham Hill. As he raised his goggles to his face, moments

Bandini's Ferrari punts Graham Hill's BRM during the 1964 Mexican Grand Prix

before the start, the elastic slipped out. Fumbling with gloved hands, he somehow fixed the problem, but had not quite completed the operation when the flag fell. Thus, at the end of the opening lap he was back in 10th place. And Surtees, with a misfire, was 13th.

Clark had no such troubles, however, rocketing away into his customary lead, followed by Gurney's Brabham and Bandini's Ferrari. With both of his rivals out of the top six, it was a promising start to the afternoon, but Graham's goggles were firmly in place and John's engine cleared its throat. Both quickly progressed through the field.

Hill's drive was particularly impressive, and after only a few laps he was into the third place he needed to be absolutely sure of the championship. But Bandini and Surtees were next in line, and Lorenzo was very keen on passing Graham.

Several times the Italian came close to punting the BRM at the hairpin – to the point that Hill angrily shook his fist. Bandini was undeterred, and the inevitable came to pass. Just before the halfway point the two cars touched, Graham's hitting the guardrail backwards. Damage to the BRM was light, but the exhaust pipes were crumpled and Hill had to stop for repairs. Way behind now, he could only hope that the Fates would strike down Clark and Surtees.

In the late stages Jimmy's car began to falter. He noticed a trail of oil at the hairpin and deliberately took a wide line, hoping against hope that it was coming from another car. But the next lap confirmed his fears: there, on his different line, was the oil. A pipe had split. With a big lead over Gurney, he tried to nurse the car to the finish. Past the pits he went to begin his last lap, to win the World Championship. But he never reappeared, stopping out on the circuit, his engine seized. Chapman's clipboard disintegrated against the tarmac . . .

For a few brief seconds, the odds were back with Hill. Gurney now led, with Bandini second and Surtees third, but John needed six points to beat Graham. To a man the Ferrari team leapt out onto the track, frantically waving Lorenzo down. It was a repeat of the Phil Hill-Mike Hawthorn syndrome at Casablanca six years earlier, and Bandini backed right off, allowing his teammate to cross the line first.

In the space of a minute, the World Championship passed through the hands of all three contenders. It was Jimmy's at the start of the last lap, Graham's half-way round it and John's at the end of it. Could anyone have written a better script? Gurney's win went unnoticed.

Surtees leading Graham Hill and Gurney, 1964 US GP at Watkins Glen

Monaco 1965

Graham Hill always counted the third of his five Monaco Grand Prix wins as perhaps the best drive of his life. It was, by any standards, a fantastic performance, the circumstances of the day making call on Hill's incredible determination, which was perhaps his greatest single attribute as a racing driver.

One factor which opened up the 1965 Monaco Grand Prix was the absence of Jimmy Clark, who was away winning $166,621 at Indianapolis. Hill's chances of a hat-trick were therefore stronger than ever, and he qualified fastest in practice, from Jack Brabham, Jackie Stewart (in the second BRM) and the Ferraris of Lorenzo Bandini and John Surtees.

Trailed by Stewart, Graham went straight into the lead, and soon the two BRMs were drawing comfortably away from the Ferraris, apparently heading for an easy afternoon. As he approached the quarter-distance mark, Hill led his partner by three seconds, with Bandini and Surtees a further 15 seconds adrift. But lap 25 changed everything.

It was all going smoothly up to that point. Then I went over the slight brow before the chicane – and found a car in the

Graham Hill, Bandini (17) and Surtees braking into Mirabeau, 1965 Monaco GP

middle of the road, virtually stopped! It was Bob Anderson, as it turned out, and his car was jammed in first gear. There were no yellow flags, nothing. I couldn't have made it through the chicane without hitting him so I had to go down the escape road, pulling up in a great cloud of tyre smoke, with the engine stalled . . .

As Stewart and the Ferraris went through, Graham jumped out of his car, pushed it back up the escape road, leapt aboard and restarted. He was now 34 seconds behind the leader, but beginning a truly wonderful drive.

It must be admitted, however, that his cause was favoured by the Fates. After only five laps in front, the inexperienced Stewart spun at Ste Devote, damaging a wheel and losing the lead to Bandini. Coming up quickly now was Brabham, who disposed of both Ferraris to move into first place, but the Australian lost his oil pressure soon afterwards. This left Bandini and Surtees at the head of the field, with the remarkable Hill now third and only four seconds adrift.

Practice, until the lunatic advent of the qualifying tyre, meant something, providing a reasonable guide to the ultimate *race* performance of each car and driver. Throughout the second half of the race the leading trio lapped at about the pace they had managed in qualifying, and for much of the time they were actually under their best practice times. Hill quickly closed in, but at Monte Carlo overtaking is rarely the work of a moment.

Realising that he could not fend off the BRM indefinitely, Surtees waved Graham through soon after the halfway mark. For another 11 laps Bandini gallantly held on at the front, but Hill was not to be denied, and passed the Ferrari under braking for Mirabeau on lap 65. Lorenzo, to his credit, did not give up, never allowing Graham to get more than three seconds ahead, but in the last few laps Surtees overtook his team-mate for the first time, intent on a final attack.

It was fruitless. For all John's efforts, the gap remained about the same, a tenth lost here, gained there. And, tragically for Surtees, his Ferrari ran out of fuel with a couple of laps left, and he was passed by Bandini and Stewart. In the end Hill won by a full minute, a triumph for courage and tenacity.

Works Lotuses at Clermont-Ferrand in 1965

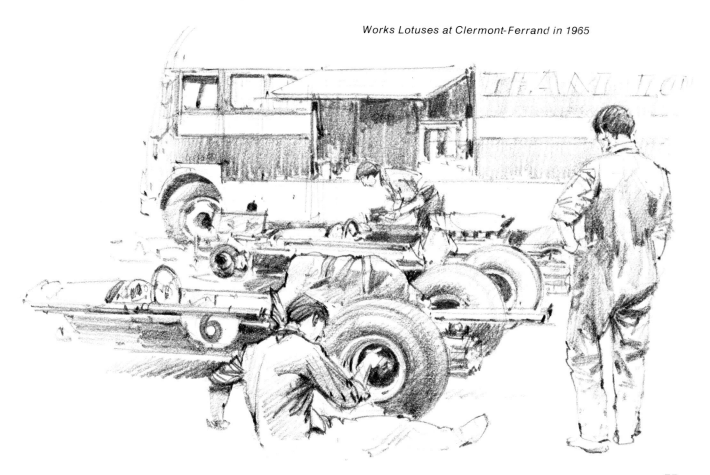

Clermont-Ferrand 1965

The supremacy of Jimmy Clark made much of the 1965 season something of a bore. Usually the only speculation before a race concerned second place, and to the other drivers that began to seem like victory. Everyone knew that Clark was going to win. Six of the first seven races fell to him, and the seventh he missed. Over the weekend of the Monaco Grand Prix Jimmy was otherwise occupied – winning the Indy 500 . . .

No victory that year came to him more easily than the French Grand Prix, held at the beautiful, mountainous circuit at Clermont-Ferrand for the first time. Clark was one of several drivers new to the track, but he swiftly came to grips with the 8-kilometre (5-mile) circuit and claimed his usual pole position. It was some measure of the promise of Jackie Stewart, then in his first Formula 1 season, that the young Scot qualified his BRM second, only half a second slower than Jimmy's Lotus 33. Third, after a banzai effort, was Lorenzo Bandini in a flat-12 Ferrari, but no one expected the young Italian to sustain this form in the race.

Clermont-Ferrand start: Clark (6), Bandini (4), Stewart (12), Gurney (14), Surtees (2) and Ginther (26, Honda)

Nor was anybody surprised when Clark took the lead at the start, with Bandini also getting away well and beating Stewart into the first corner. The Ferrari was still second at the end of the first lap, but Stewart, Gurney and Surtees were all pressing hard, and it was clear that Lorenzo was holding them up.

This had no great bearing on the outcome of the race, however, for the 1965 French Grand Prix was one of those which simply surrendered itself to Clark from the outset. After a single lap the Lotus led by more than three seconds; after two the gap was six seconds, and now Stewart had moved into the runner-up position, where he remained for the rest of the race. Surtees moved past his Ferrari team-mate into third spot, and there he stayed until the fall of the flag. Denny Hulme's Brabham was an equally constant fourth.

Despite easing off considerably in the closing laps, Clark was still almost half a minute to the good when he crossed the finishing line. By this time most of the spectators were yawning. Why did they call this thing *racing?* Genius had made a joke of it.

Monaco 1966

Jimmy Clark

It was a messy opening race of the new 3-litre Formula 1, for a ragbag of machinery was gathered together in Monaco. As always at the beginning of a new formula, few teams were ready, neither Honda nor Eagle even making the trip to the Principality. Cooper, however, had 3-litre V12 Maserati-powered cars for Jochen Rindt and Richie Ginther, and Jack Brabham had his Repco V8-engined car. For John Surtees there was a new 3-litre V12 Ferrari.

Other leading runners had to compromise, Lotus and BRM, for example, fielding what were essentially 1965 cars with engines stretched to 2-litres. Perhaps the best compromise of all was Lorenzo Bandini's Ferrari, less cumbersome than the new car at a tight circuit like this, and fitted with a 2.4-litre V6 engine. Surtees, recognising its potential for Monaco, was keen to drive it, but team manager Eugenio Dragoni insisted that it be assigned to his Italian protegé . . .

During practice Monte Carlo was like a town under siege. In addition to all the usual hold-ups and disruptions, there was the making of the film *Grand Prix* to consider. Practice schedules counted for nothing in the face of Hollywood. Protests were silenced in time-

honoured style: a dog will not howl if you beat him with a bone.

In the midst of all this there was practice, from which Jimmy Clark emerged as pole position man. Surtees, working on equal parts of inspiration and anger, coaxed the new Ferrari onto the front row, and the BRMs of Stewart and Hill were next up.

Clark's customary Monaco luck did not dally in appearing this time. Jimmy got off the line well enough, reached for the lever to snatch second – and found that first would not disengage. Eventually he freed it, selected second and tore off up the hill, by now 16th and last.

There were no such problems for Surtees, however, the Ferrari taking the lead immediately, followed by Stewart, Hulme and the remarkable Bob Anderson, who had qualified eighth in his Brabham-Climax.

Surtees held tenuous sway at the front for 14 laps before the Ferrari's differential expired, and Stewart moved into a lead which was his for the afternoon. The only possible threat appeared to be Clark, who was making fantastic progress through the field – 16th on lap one, seventh on lap eight! By now, though, Jimmy had lost an enormous amount of time in the traffic. He eventually got as high as fourth before the Lotus' rear suspension collapsed . . .

In the late stages the circuit was almost deserted, but Bandini stirred up a little interest by starting to catch Stewart, little by little. The Scot was clearly paying out line, well in control of the situation, but Lorenzo's showing was impressive. With 10 laps left he put in a remarkable lap which was faster even than Clark's pole position time, but thereafter his brakes began to go away, and JYS took his second Grand Prix victory by a comfortable 40 seconds. Only four cars were classified!

Jackie Stewart in the 1966 Monaco Grand Prix

Spa 1966

John Frankenheimer's film *Grand Prix* received mixed notices from the cognoscenti when it was released early in 1967. The plot, it was agreed, was thin, and so were most of the characters. But Frankenheimer brought Hollywood technique and skills to the art of filming racing cars in action, and for that the sport must be grateful. Today the movie bears re-viewing, partly out of nostalgia for those days of BRDC badges and unsponsored cars, partly because it constitutes a record of the 1966 Formula 1 season.

Perhaps Frankenheimer's timing was not of the best. He chose, after all, the first year of a new formula, which inevitably meant that grids were a *mélange* of machinery: something old, something new, something borrowed, something blue . . . There was a little of everything.

In June they came together at Spa, when everything pointed to a victory for John Surtees and Ferrari. As ever, when it came to being ready for a new formula, Maranello was ahead of the game. While many rival

teams messed around with stretched engines from the previous 1.5-litre Formula 1, Ferrari were ready with a new 3-litre V12. Jack Brabham had his reliable, if somewhat underpowered, 3-litre V8 Repco engine, and John Cooper's cars used Maserati V12 units based on that run unsuccessfully by the factory nine years earlier. Other than those, the only 'full-size' engine on display early in 1966 was the woefully complicated and unreliable BRM H16.

On paper, then, Spa was for Surtees, recently back in the cockpit after a near-fatal accident in a CanAm race the previous autumn. John was driving as well as ever, and this daunting, swerving snake of a road through the Ardennes held no fears for him. Spa was a circuit unforgiving of error, but Surtees was a man who made few driving mistakes, and Ferrari a company whose cars rarely broke. Psychologically, therefore, Big John was better equipped than most to deal with perhaps the most lethal track in the world, and he took pole position without difficulty, with Jochen Rindt's Cooper-Maserati and Jackie Stewart's BRM next up.

No matter who you were, how great your ability, if you were a Grand Prix driver, you shuddered on the morning of June 12. It was race day, and it was overcast. Spa in the rain was always a terrifying prospect.

At the fall of the flag, however, the road was dry, and Surtees led Rindt, Brabham, Bandini and Stewart through Eau Rouge and away up the hill. Once at the top, at the left-handed Les Combes, the Ferrari began the helter-skelter plunge down to Burnenville, Malmédy and Masta — and there the chaos began. On that section of the circuit rain had been falling for several minutes. At dry speeds, the cars suddenly found a wet surface . . .

Spence, Hulme, Siffert and Bonnier all went off at Malmédy, the Swede's Cooper-Maserati coming to rest on top of a bridge, teetering. At the Masta Curve all three BRMs went out of control, Stewart being trapped, injured, in the wreckage of his, while colleagues Graham Hill and Bob Bondurant gallantly laboured to free him.

Thus it was that only seven cars came round at the

Cooper on the Monaco grid, 1966

end of the first lap: Surtees – ten seconds – Brabham – Bandini – ten seconds – Ginther – Rindt – Ligier – Gurney. What terrible thing, they wondered in the pits, could have happened out there? Word eventually filtered back that, mercifully, no one was seriously hurt, but Spa's future as a Grand Prix circuit was already sealed. From then on, Jackie Stewart, his collarbone broken, would campaign ceaselessly for its removal from the World Championship schedule.

The race itself became a straight fight between Surtees and Rindt. Very much the *enfant terrible* of motor racing at that time, Jochen drove as great a race that day as any in his career. He, too, had gone out of control on that first lap, the Cooper-Maserati pirouetting six times before its disbelieving driver could collect his thoughts, realising that somehow he had not hit a thing. Thereafter he chased after Surtees with such vigour that he took the lead on lap four!

For nearly two hours Rindt kept in front, making full call on his freakish reflexes. And all the while Surtees and the Ferrari kept in touch, stalking. With five laps to go the gap was only a couple of seconds, and now John made his move. At the same time the differential in Jochen's car began to play up, and he could no longer sustain the pace. At the finish he was more than 40 seconds behind.

And we have Frankenheimer to thank for putting on record one of the great *mano-a-mano* battles of racing history, a day when guile and control were balanced with heroism.

'Old Man' Jack Brabham teases the press at Zandvoort

Reims 1966

Reims marked the start of Jack Brabham's Indian Summer. Since winning the World Championship in 1959 and 1960, the Australian had been through a lean time. He had remained competitive, had won the odd non-Championship race, but when he came to Reims in 1966 he was almost six years from his last Grand Prix victory.

There were changes in the order of things at the French Grand Prix. A fortnight before, at Le Mans, John Surtees had finally split from Ferrari after more intolerable treatment from team manager Dragoni.

That was a turning point in my life, I suppose, John recalls. *There was nothing extraordinary about Dragoni's behaviour at Le Mans. It was merely the place where he chose to play his cards. But I have certain convictions about the way I go through life, and there was just no way I was going to continue on that basis. My problems were only with him, really. I always had a good relationship with Bandini, despite the fact that Dragoni always favoured him. In fact, Lorenzo pleaded with me not to leave. But I never got on well with Parkes, who made no bones about the fact that he was after my drive. The Ferrari people completely miscalculated the value of their product. They thought they could win with anybody driving . . . I quickly got in touch with Cooper, and I went to Reims in a very determined frame of mind, believe me.*

Indeed he did. In the first two practice sessions John's Cooper-Maserati set the best time, but Bandini's Ferrari went faster still in the final one. Third fastest was Mike

Parkes, so Surtees would sit in the middle of the front row, sandwiched between two Ferraris. His determination went up another notch.

In that opening year of the 3-litre Formula 1, there was an odd mix of machinery, and some teams were still running 2-litre cars, which could not hope to figure at the flat-out Reims triangle. Ferrari, Cooper and Brabham were the only teams in serious contention, with Bandini the logical favourite. Jimmy Clark was a non-starter, having been hit in the face by a bird during the second day's practice, so Pedro Rodriguez took his place in the Lotus.

It is a cruel world. All John Surtees' hopes evaporated within a few seconds of the start. He got away superbly and led the field through the first corner, but the fuel pump drive sheared after only a few hundred yards, allowing Bandini into the lead. In the pits Dragoni beamed.

When the Ferrari came by at the end of the first lap it had a green car in its slipstream. Brabham had nothing like the horsepower of the Italian, but he found it possible to hang on to him. Gradually, very gradually, Bandini inched away, but after only a couple of laps Parkes had been dropped. Only two men were in this race.

Lorenzo drove a splendid race that day, certainly using the Ferrari. On lap 31, with 17 to go, he led by more than half a minute. On lap 32 he did not appear. In the pits Dragoni stopped beaming. And Surtees started . . .

The luckless Bandini had stopped at Thillois with a broken throttle cable, which he temporarily repaired in order to get the Ferrari back to the pits. With a new cable he rejoined in a selfless attempt to tow Parkes up to Brabham. By this time, however, Jack led by nearly a minute, and Ferrari's position was hopeless. Although he backed right off in the last few laps Brabham won comfortably, to the delight of the crowd. As has been chronicled many times, this was the first time a driver ever won a Grand Prix in a car bearing his own name, and it gave Jack a renewed taste for victory. In the following weeks he also won at Brands Hatch, the Nürburgring and Zandvoort on his way to a third World Championship.

As for Reims, the 1966 Grand Prix was the last. Financial troubles were eating away at the organising club, and racing at the celebrated track ceased altogether in 1969. The pits and the grandstand now make up a crumbling, ghostly memento of great times past.

Monaco 1967

Denny Hulme is one of motor racing's 'forgotten' World Champions, a man who positively detested the limelight, who won the title in 1967 simply because he happened to come out of the season with more points than anyone else. You got the impression that it was just one of those things.

Hulme's driving matched his personality. It was gritty and understated, rarely exciting, usually effective. For Denny, motor racing was not a romantic thing, and winning was something to be done by the simplest means possible.

It is odd, therefore, that his first Grand Prix victory was so totally unlike those which followed. Anyone who was at Monte Carlo in 1967 witnessed an exhibition of flamboyant car control such as has rarely been seen through the Principality's famous streets. Arm-twirling, opposite lock, power slides were what took Hulme to victory that afternoon in early May.

Sadly for the New Zealander, the race is remembered not for his impressive win but for one of the most appallingly gruesome accidents in the sport's history. As Denny stepped up to meet the Rainiers, black smoke

wafted over the harbour and out into the infinity of the ocean. A few laps from the end Lorenzo Bandini's Ferrari, chasing Hulme for first place, had crashed at the chicane, somersaulted and exploded into flame. The handsome Italian was trapped in the upturned car for five minutes, and was eventually taken to hospital with horrifying burns. He died three days later.

Bandini was the matinee idol of the motor racing *tifosi*. He was Ferrari team leader, and his season had started superbly. Second at Monaco in 1965 and '66, he was sure that this was his year. So confident of winning was he, indeed, that he bought a new dinner jacket for the Monaco weekend, something suitable for the traditional post-race Gala at the Hôtel de Paris. By Sunday evening, though, he was fighting for his life in the hospital, and the Gala was cancelled. No one felt like celebrating, least of all Denny Hulme.

Everyone felt a lot of sympathy for Denny, who had driven a perfect race. In the early laps he was unable to keep pace with Jackie Stewart's BRM, but when the Scot retired he moved the Brabham into a lead it kept all afternoon. Second, chasing that elusive win, ran Bandini. In the heat of the day the slim Italian was ill-equipped to deal with the bullish Hulme, as the Ferrari, for all its horsepower advantage, was a big and cumbersome car for a tight circuit.

Chris Amon, making his Formula 1 debut for Ferrari, ran third. *I'm pretty sure Lorenzo crashed because of fatigue. I reckon he must have been terribly tired – he was going quicker than I was, and I was completely spent. The Ferrari was a handful at Monte Carlo, and I was stronger than he was, anyway. Then you'd see Denny in the Brabham, and it was like a Formula 3 car! He just gave the impression that he could go on indefinitely like that . . .*

So, it seemed, he could. Bandini crashed after 82 of the 100 laps, and there was no move to stop the race, although burning fuel and wreckage littered the track, and passing cars hindered the pitiful attempts to rescue the trapped man. There was no fire-proof clothing for the marshals, and so Bandini burned to death before them. It was hideous and disgraceful.

In victory, Hulme stood with the trophy, looking at the ground, scuffing his feet. His first Grand Prix was won, and he felt both exhilarated and wretched.

Zandvoort 1967

In 1967 the teams went to Zandvoort in a subdued frame of mind. Fresh in everyone's memory was the cruel death of Lorenzo Bandini, at Monte Carlo a month earlier. Marshals in silver suits were much in evidence at the Dutch circuit.

Jimmy Clark went to Zandvoort intrigued and a little apprehensive, for he had never so much as seen the car he was to drive. The Lotus 49, complete with new Cosworth DFV engine, was making its first appearance, and Jimmy, thanks to his country's punitive tax laws, was unwillingly living abroad for a while. As was his custom, the Scot drove from his Paris apartment to Holland in his yellow Elan.

What he found there was the beginning of a new era, albeit in somewhat rough and ready form. Quite clearly the Cosworth engine had a good deal more horsepower than any other of the time, but in original form it did not make life easy for the driver, the bulk of

the power arriving with a bang at around 6,500 revs. In behaviour, then, it was rather like an early F1 turbocharged engine: it delivered the goods, but you had to be ready for them. Even for a driver of Clark's genius, that took a little adjustment. As well as that, the early 49 chassis tended to be somewhat wilful, so the whole package required enormous skill to exploit its potential.

In practice Jimmy was prepared to take his time, settling for eighth place on the grid, while team-mate Graham Hill, who had done all the testing and knew the car's little ways, put his 49 on pole position, half a second clear of Gurney's Eagle-Weslake.

There was much at stake as the cars lined up on the grid that overcast afternoon. Ford had paid Keith Duckworth £100,000 to design and build this new engine, whose cam covers bore their name, and many of the company's top men were on hand to watch its debut. They permitted themselves a small grin apiece when Hill led the field by two clear seconds at the end of the opening lap, but winced when he clattered into the pits with camshaft problems only 10 laps later.

Clark, in the meantime, was getting the hang of the 49. Sixth at the start, he had calmly picked off Amon's Ferrari and moved up to fourth when Gurney retired. Now, with Hill going out, he assumed third place and began to catch Rindt and Brabham, dealing with them effortlessly on consecutive laps. And thereafter he simply drove away for a remarkable debut victory for the Lotus 49 and the Cosworth DFV.

For the Ford men, it was an afternoon of unbearable tension which ended in joy and relief. As they left Zandvoort that day every rival team knew that its engines were no longer competitive, and that if the DFV held together it would dominate everywhere. That, in fact, became the story of the season. When Clark finished, he invariably won. By year's end he would have four Grand Prix victories, yet would lose the World Championship to a man with only a couple, for Denny Hulme and the Brabham-Repco were nearly always in the points.

A crystal ball could have saved the Ford executives a lot of grief. It could have told them that their money was well spent, that the DFV would be winning 15 years hence, and beyond. At the time of writing, each Grand Prix victory has cost Ford exactly £657.89p. It seems like a fair return on their money . . .

Spa 1967

Dan Gurney came to Spa in 1967 fresh from his victory at Le Mans. He and A. J. Foyt had led virtually all the way in their 7-litre Ford, and everyone agreed that there never was a less likely driver partnership to last 24 hours! Still, the two chargers did the job perfectly, and the car ran like a clock. *I can't believe it!* said Daniel Sexton Gurney afterwards, *Why, I'll be winning a Grand Prix next . . .*

The 1967 season was Gurney's ninth as a Grand Prix driver, yet he had remarkably little to show for it. As a driver, pure and simple, he was the man whom Jimmy Clark most feared, yet he had only three Grand Prix victories against his name. And most doubted the wisdom of his decision to form his own team in 1966. That first season, using antiquated Climax engines in his Eagle chassis, had been shambolic, but now the Weslake V12 was ready, and Dan had already won the Race of Champions with it. The blue and white car was a gorgeous thing to behold and made a sublime sound – but could it win Grands Prix?

At Spa Gurney set the second best practice time, behind the inevitable Clark. Unlike Jimmy, he loved the Ardennes circuit and had completely dominated the 1964 event before running out of fuel on the last lap. Now, three years later, he had a good feeling about the race.

For all that, his start was disastrous. When the flag went down he was not in gear, and as the field streamed away up the hill the Eagle was somewhere in midfield. By the end of the first lap Gurney was up to fifth place, but Clark's leading Lotus 49 was already 10 seconds ahead.

Jackie Stewart had the H-16 BRM up in second place, but the controversial Bourne car had already been the cause of a major accident, which ended the brief Formula 1 career of Mike Parkes. The Englishman's Ferrari was running fourth, behind the BRM and ahead of team-mate Chris Amon. The New Zealander saw the whole thing and, coming just a month after Lorenzo Bandini's fatal accident at Monaco, admits that it shook him.

The BRMs were always dumping oil all over the place, and Jackie's car just emptied its catch tank onto the road. I was right behind Mike, saw him go and backed off, but it still gave me a hell of a moment. I must say that it upset me a lot. I saw most of the accident in my mirrors after I'd gone through, and it was just like a toy car rolling along the bank. It was way up in the air, and then I saw him getting thrown out. I just couldn't see how he might have survived. It had a very profound effect on me, and I think it totally destroyed poor old Scarfiotti. He'd already gone through a real crisis of confidence after Lorenzo's death, and I don't think he ever drove well in Formula 1 afterwards.

Parkes escaped with his life, but had dreadful leg injuries and never drove a Grand Prix car again.

Clark ran away with the race until lap 13 when he came in to have the Cosworth's plugs changed, one of them having broken up. And two laps later he was back with exactly the same problem. Stewart, who had run second from the beginning, took over the lead for a while, but Jackie had gear selection problems in the BRM, and soon he was having to hold the lever at all times. As he laconically remarked afterwards, Spa is quite daunting enough with two hands, let alone one . . .

A few laps earlier, Gurney had been briefly into the pits to express concern about low fuel pressure from the Weslake engine, but he continued after a few seconds, still in second place, and really put the hammer down,

gaining on Stewart and passing him with eight laps to go. At the flag he was more than a minute clear of the BRM, with Amon third and Jochen Rindt's Cooper-Maserati fourth.

Dan's expression was joyous as he threw flowers to the crowd afterwards. After all those years of toil everything seemed to be coming right for him. Sadly, though, neither he nor his team was ever to win another Grand Prix, and soon they were gone from the scene.

Silverstone 1967

From the beginning of practice the issue was never really in doubt. Silverstone would conform to the 1967 pattern: if the Lotuses held together, they would walk away. With two great drivers and a terrific power advantage from the new Cosworth DFV engine it was unlikely that Colin Chapman's cars would be chal-

lenged. Predictably, Jimmy Clark and Graham Hill took the first two positions on the grid, followed by the Brabhams of Jack himself and Denny Hulme, Gurney's Eagle and Amon's Ferrari.

The battle for the front was not exciting, for Clark and Hill soon detached themselves from the pack and

motored away to swap the lead. Graham eventually retired with broken rear suspension, leaving Jimmy to stroll home.

Clark's visit to Britain was necessarily a short one, for 1967 was the year of his self-imposed tax exile. Only a fleeting visit was possible and this, tragically, was the last time he was ever to set foot in his own country.

As the Lotus superiority was so obvious and Hulme's third place similarly comfortable, it was good for the spectators that there was a tremendous battle for fourth which lasted for virtually the whole of the race: Brabham versus Amon. Time after time the Ferrari would flick out of Jack's slipstream, only to fall back into line again. Amon recalls that race with pleasure.

The Ferrari handled nicely, but we were not very competitive on horsepower, and the thing was terribly heavy. That was my first season with Ferrari, and for nearly all of it I was the only driver. I kept telling Mauro Forghieri that we were slow in a straight line, and it was a long time before he believed me. That's the trouble with 12-cylinder engines: they make this lovely, loud, powerful noise! But that doesn't mean *they're shoving much out . . .*

That race at Silverstone, though, was one of the most enjoyable I ever had. The Lotuses were in another race, we all knew that, so the best thing to do was just forget they were there at all. I got involved in this big dice with old Jack, and I remember he was adjusting his mirrors early in the race – and one of them flew off and whistled past my head! Then he seemed to be adjusting the other one . . . I've never been quite sure whether he was adjusting them or trying to tear them off . . .

After about 30 laps he'd lost both mirrors, and then we had a real tussle. That was a very wide car indeed, but of course afterwards he tells me he's very sorry for chopping me all over the place but his mirrors were gone and he didn't know I was there!

I finally passed him out of Woodcote with about four laps to go. He went a bit wide there and I was able to get a run at him down to Copse. But he did a good job, I must say. After I got him I closed a lot on Denny in the other Brabham, but there just wasn't time to catch him. I finished third.

It was a real old-fashioned dice I had with Jack, and that

93

was why it was so enjoyable. He was throwing everything in the bloody book at me – stones, grass, dirt, everything! Then, of course, we went to the Nürburgring a couple of weeks later and had a repeat performance! There were some good days that summer . . .

Rouen 1968

After a disastrous visit to the 'Bugatti' circuit at Le Mans in 1967 (where the competitors almost outnumbered the spectators), the next French Grand Prix was staged at Rouen, a magnificent, if dangerous, circuit which was a true test of the racing driver.

Many drivers admitted to a sense of foreboding when they arrived for the race, for the sport was going through a particularly tragic time. In the recent past Jimmy Clark had died at Hockenheim on April 7, Mike Spence at Indianapolis on May 7 and Lodovico Scarfiotti at Rossfeld on June 8. Now, a further month on, came Rouen, with the race to be run on July 7.

The established aces of the day – Rindt, Stewart, Ickx, Amon, Surtees and so on – duly qualified for the quick end of the grid. However, at the back were two complete newcomers to Formula 1: Vic Elford, already established as a superb rally and sports car driver, in a works Cooper-BRM, and Jo Schlesser, realising his life's ambition by finally competing in a Grand Prix at the age of 40.

Schlesser's entry was a controversial one, despite the fact that his ability was proven, for the Frenchman was nominated to drive the new Honda RA302. The car, with new air-cooled V8 engine, had been tested briefly in England by the company's regular driver, John Surtees, who pronounced it promising, but most definitely not ready to race. Honda decided to ignore John's words and handed the car over to their French division, then involved in a major marketing drive and consequently keen to have a French-driven Honda run in the French Grand Prix. Jo Schlesser was unable to turn down the opportunity, and Surtees washed his hands of the whole affair.

As they prepared for the start in the late afternoon light rain began to fall and everyone ruminated about tyres, most opting for intermediates, with Jacky Ickx choosing wets. The Belgian's decision was to prove crucial. In the course of the first lap the rain came down harder, and the pattern of the day was set.

Stewart's Matra led initially, but Ickx had taken the Ferrari to the front before the end of the first lap and came by the pits with a lead of two seconds. Already thrusting their way through were Surtees and Pedro Rodriguez, both hard men, both excellent in the wet.

On lap three came the chaos. Going down through the endless sequence of fast sweepers towards the Nouveau Monde hairpin, Schlesser's engine suddenly cut out completely. With no drive, the Honda ran wide, understeering off the road and into a steep bank, whereupon it immediately exploded. Much of the car's chassis was of magnesium, which served only to make the conflagration worse. That, combined with a full fuel load, made for a colossal fire, which spread right across the road, leaving other drivers no alternative but to drive through it. The race was not stopped. There

was, of course, no chance at all for poor Schlesser, and several spectators were also burned.

At the front, however, the battle continued, Rodriguez actually getting past Ickx briefly, despite having only intermediate tyres! But then the rain came down torrentially for a while, allowing the Ferrari driver to pull well clear. In a matter of eight laps he stretched his lead to a minute.

As afternoon went into evening the circuit began to dry, and a glimmer of sun emerged. By this time Surtees had been delayed with a pit stop to change smashed goggles and Rodriguez to have a punctured tyre replaced. Ickx, regular as ever, had an advantage of two minutes when he took the flag for his first Grand Prix win. But it was a joyless day, and Grand Prix cars never went back to Rouen.

Spa 1968

Bruce McLaren knew all about Spa. He had been competing in Belgian Grands Prix there since 1960, and once, in 1964, he had very nearly won. When Gurney's Brabham ran out of fuel on the last lap Bruce's Cooper had inherited the lead – only to suffer the same fate right at the end of the lap. Still it seemed that the New Zealander would freewheel down from La Source and make it to the line first, but with mere yards to go Jimmy Clark swooped past for the victory. In 1968, the luck was with McLaren.

The race did not begin promisingly for him. At the end of the first lap the yellow M7A was in 11th place, already 13 seconds down on the leader. McLaren had not won a Grand Prix for six years at this time, although he had conclusively dominated the Race of Champions at Brands Hatch a few weeks earlier.

Practice had belonged to Chris Amon's Ferrari, which took pole position by some four seconds from Jackie Stewart's Matra. For this race the Italian team was trying something new: a rear wing. Amon reckoned that this undoubtedly improved the car's stability through Spa's ultra-fast swerves, but teammate Jacky Ickx was not convinced. For the race the Belgian decided to run without the wing.

By the end of the first lap Amon led convincingly from John Surtees in the Honda, but it all went wrong for the Ferrari driver on lap two . . .

Jo Bonnier had some problems with his McLaren, and he

was limping back, still on his first lap. I came up on him just after the Masta Kink, and had to back right off to miss him. That let Surtees close up on me, and he went past me on the straight. That was a shame for me because I'd just about dropped him before then, and the Honda was way quicker in a straight line than the Ferrari. After that I was all over him through the corners, but he'd blow me away down the straight. It was very annoying, I must say, but it didn't last that long. After about eight laps one of his wheels flicked up a stone which went straight through my oil radiator, so that was the end of that.

Only a couple of laps later Surtees, too, was out, after a breakage in the Honda's rear suspension, and Denny Hulme's McLaren moved into first place, tailed by Stewart. The Matra soon took over, but Denny did not surrender easily, and for a time these two put on a spectacular duel which ended when the McLaren broke a driveshaft.

Stewart was now set for a second consecutive victory at Spa. McLaren was in second place, but well over half a minute behind.

As had happened in 1967, however, Jackie's victory hopes evaporated towards the end. At the beginning of the last lap he brought the Matra slowly into the pits, out of fuel. Bruce flashed through to lead the only lap that matters, and crossed the line 12 seconds ahead of Pedro Rodriguez's BRM.

There was no Belgian Grand Prix in 1969, but in

McLaren, Rodriguez and Courage approach Stavelot at Spa in 1968

1970 they came back to Spa. This time Rodriguez won, but no one really felt like going racing. Just five days before Bruce McLaren had been killed, testing his new CanAm car at Goodwood.

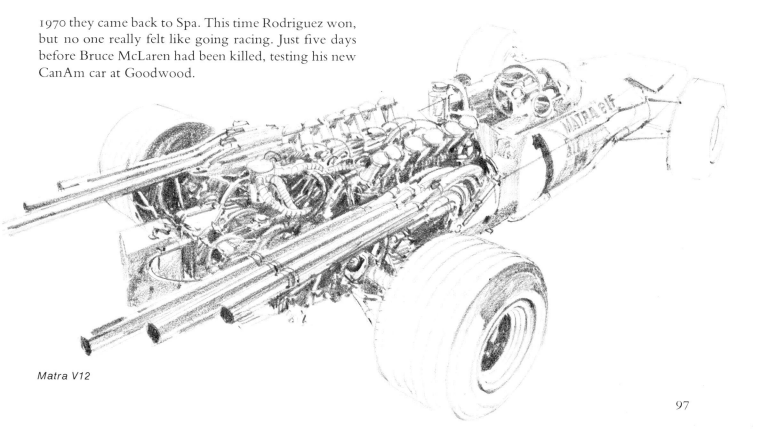

Matra V12

Zandvoort 1968

Talk of Jackie Stewart in the rain always brings to mind his extraordinary drive at the Nürburgring in 1968, where, in truly atrocious conditions, he won the German Grand Prix by four clear minutes. The enormity of that feat tends to dwarf his other wet victory of that year, in the Dutch Grand Prix at Zandvoort.

The Scot was in low spirits when he arrived in Holland. This was his first season with Ken Tyrrell's Formula 1 team (itself new to Grand Prix racing), and the first four races of Jackie's year had yielded only three championship points. The team was running a Cosworth-powered Matra MS10, and the car was not quite on the pace. In addition, Stewart had broken a bone in his wrist after crashing in a Formula 2 car at Jarama. For many weeks it was in plaster, and caused him considerable pain, exacerbated by the undulations of Zandvoort. In practice Jackie was fifth fastest, behind Amon (Ferrari), Rindt (Brabham), Hill (Lotus) and Brabham. He did not look to the race with confidence.

The weather changed everything. Shortly before the start it began to drizzle, leaving everyone in a quandary. Wet or dry tyres? Most opted to stay on dries, for the sky was brightening, but Stewart went for dries with a hand-cut drainage channel in the centre.

After only a few laps there was a torrential downpour, and Jackie could have hoped for nothing better. Dunlops indubitably had a huge advantage in the rain. By lap four the Matra was in the lead, and going away by at least a second a lap. It appeared that Stewart was under no threat at all, but then the progress of Jean-Pierre Beltoise came sharply into focus . . .

The Frenchman was at the wheel of the factory Matra MS11, this powered by the company's own V12 engine. Prior to this race the car had been something of an embarrassment to Matra, for it was never close to the Tyrrell-run Cosworth car. Now, however, it was bellowing its glorious sound to some purpose. Beltoise was on Dunlop wets, and the smooth 12-cylinder power was a further boon in the conditions. Jean-Pierre had qualified only 16th, but was up to third after only four laps! In no time he had passed Hill for second, and actually began to close on Stewart . . .

Jackie, however, drove faultlessly, and there lay the difference, for Beltoise had two spins, one of which left his car with sand in the throttle slides. After a pit stop he

rejoined in seventh place, but quickly moved up to second once more. Now, however, he was a little more circumspect, and there were no further mistakes.

It was a long, long afternoon, with Stewart coming in to win after 2 hours and 46 minutes of racing. Beltoise was a minute and a half behind, and these two alone went the full distance. The importance of Dunlop's contribution may be judged by the fact that Rodriguez and Ickx, brilliant rain drivers both, finished third and fourth, lapped by both the Matras. Pedro was on Goodyears, Jacky on Firestones.

I look back on that win with a lot of pleasure, says Stewart, *because I feel that it was a race I wasn't meant to win. Various things came together which enabled me to steal it, if you like. Our car and tyres were always good in the rain that year. If it had been dry on race day there is no way I could have run with Chrissie and Jochen. No way. Not even if my arm had been OK. And, to be quite honest, if it had been dry I just would not have been able to go the distance, let alone win the race. As it was, my arm gave me a lot of pain, but at dry roads speeds it would have been too much . . .*

Brands Hatch 1968

I suppose, said Rob Walker, *that winning that day at Brands – the British Grand Prix, after all – meant more to me than any other victory my team ever had. And what an exciting race! I was very proud of Seppi that day. The only thing that made me a little bit sad was that we won at Chris's expense . . .*

The 1968 British Grand Prix was, indeed, an exciting race. Practice had indicated that the car to have was a Lotus 49, with the factory cars of Graham Hill and Jack Oliver first and second on the grid, and Jo Siffert's Walker-entered car fourth. The only likely challenge seemed to be from Chris Amon's V12 Ferrari, third. The New Zealander had been close to victory several times, and he hoped that race day at Brands – also his 25th birthday – would bring an end to his extremely evil luck.

After HRH Prince Charles had arrived by helicopter and the Red Arrows had done their usual stunning routine, out came the cars. The morning had been dull, and now there was very light drizzle, which prompted some teams to put their cars on rain tyres. Ferrari decided to hedge their bets, leaving Amon's car alone while putting Jacky Ickx's on intermediates.

All the Lotuses stayed with dry tyres, and it was the right decision for the spots of rain ceased, and soon the sun emerged. Hill and Oliver led confidently from the start, with Siffert slotting into third, ahead of Amon. After 10 laps it was obvious that this was a four-car race, for Jackie Stewart's Matra, leading the rest, was being left behind.

Colin Chapman's plans began to go awry on lap 26 when Hill retired with a broken driveshaft. But Oliver, at his favourite circuit, calmly took over at the front,

and Amon passed Siffert for second place, regained by Seppi a few laps later.

As the blue Lotus snicked by the Ferrari the battle became important, for Oliver's engine expired. The fight for third, then second, was now for the lead. Amon remembers it well.

I think wings were the decisive factor that day. Lotus were just starting to use that huge rear-mounted thing, whereas we had a smaller, centre-mounted, one, which didn't give anything like as much downforce. I loved that '68 Ferrari more than any other car I ever drove – you could do anything with it, and sideways was the quickest way, which I always enjoyed. I think, without a doubt, that it was the best chassis of that season, but the V12 was just blown away by the Cosworths. Funny, really, when you think that Ferraris usually have lots of horsepower and lousy chassis . . .

When Oliver retired, the race had 36 laps to run, and for most of the way Siffert and Amon ran together, the Lotus pulling out on the straights, the Ferrari clawing back through the corners. It was a totally absorbing duel, resolved ultimately by the disintegration of the Italian car's rear tyres.

I just plain ran out of rubber during the last few laps, recalls Chris. *The Lotuses worked really well at Brands, and I got left behind out of the slow corners. I was disappointed afterwards, of course, but not dissatisfied, because I'd driven balls to the wall all the way. I remember that the Ferrari people were a bit annoyed with me for not winning – until they saw the tyres! Then they were a bit more understanding . . .*

At the flag Siffert was a little over four seconds in front. It was his first Grand Prix victory, and the last to be won by Rob Walker's team.

Mexico 1968

The 1968 World Championship, like many before it, hung on the outcome of the final race. Graham Hill, Jackie Stewart and Denny Hulme all went off to Mexico in November with title hopes. Stewart, without any doubt, was the best driver of the three, but most of the sentiment was with Hill, who alone had kept Lotus going in the aftermath of Jimmy Clark's death early in the season.

Practice, though, did not feature any member of the championship trio. On pole position was Jo Siffert in Rob Walker's Lotus 49, with the Ferrari of Chris Amon next to him. Hill and Hulme made up the second row, but Stewart was back on the fourth.

On race day it mattered not, for Siffert and Amon both made poor starts, and Hill took the lead immediately, followed by Surtees (Honda), Stewart, Amon and Hulme. By lap five Jackie had the Tyrrell-run

Matra in first place, with Graham right on his tail and Denny third! The three contenders, therefore, held sway at the front of the field. After only 10 laps, however, Hulme was wiped from the equation, his McLaren sliding into a crash barrier after breaking a damper.

Soon Hill had the lead back from Stewart, but Siffert was going faster than either, charging along after his slow start. By quarter-distance the Swiss had taken the dark blue 49 into the lead, but had to stop shortly afterwards with a broken throttle cable.

There were no distractions now. It was Hill against Stewart, for the race and the World Championship, and the two of them circulated together until soon after the halfway mark when the Matra suddenly fell away with low fuel pressure. Jackie kept going to the end, but at the flag was back in seventh place, out of the points.

Graham Hill leads Stewart, Rindt, Amon, Surtees and Siffert, 1968 Mexican Grand Prix

So Hill sailed on for what appeared to be a serene and straightforward victory, but it was not quite as it seemed. He remembered it thus: *That was a really good race. I had quite a dice with Stewart for a while until he fell back, and also, of course, Seppi was giving me a bit of trouble until his pit stop. And I had my problems, too. This was the time of the high wings, of course, and for this race we'd devised a scheme whereby we could flatten the wing going down the straight. I had an extra pedal over the top of the clutch, and after I'd finished changing gear I'd press this pedal and put the wing flat. That gave me quite a bit of extra speed on the straight. Then, when I took my foot off the pedal, the wing snapped back into the right position for the corners.*

Now, that was all right as long as it was working properly, but soon after the start of the race I felt this pedal go light, and I saw in my mirrors that one of the two rubber straps – which operated this system – had broken. The World Championship, therefore, rested on a single rubber strap . . . That one, fortunately, held together, but it seemed like an endless race. Luckily there was no pressure on me after Jackie fell back, and I think we won by over a minute in the end . . .

Barcelona 1969

When I look back on my career now, I can remember some days of which I'm proud, some races when everything went perfectly, when the car and myself did everything right. But that win in Barcelona in '69 embarrassed me, really, because I didn't 'win' it, as such. If anything, I stole it . . .

Jackie Stewart, in harness with his favourite racing car, the Matra MS80, should have been a logical favourite for the 1969 Spanish Grand Prix. Run for the first time around the beautiful circuit in Montjuich Park, up in the hills above Barcelona, the race seemed

Stewart, Brabham, Ickx and Amon, 1969 Spanish Grand Prix

ideal for what was undoubtedly the nimblest Formula 1 car of its time.

In practice, however, Stewart was unable to match the pace of the factory Lotus 49s, driven by Jochen Rindt and Graham Hill, and the lone Ferrari 312 of Chris Amon. On race day the story was the same, Rindt and Amon leaving the rest behind in the early laps.

Montjuich was a spooky place, particularly the section immediately after the pits area. There the cars crested a rise at well over 240 kmh (150 mph) and frequently got airborne, landing on a steep downhill stretch with a hairpin at the bottom.

This was the era of the high wing, one of Grand Prix racing's periodic absurdities. In principle, as pioneered by Ferrari, the idea was fine, for the wings undoubtedly gave downforce – or 'negative lift', to quote the smart parlance of the time – and raised cornering speeds. Unfortunately, the supports on which they were mounted were not always substantial enough for the job in hand . . .

Lotus had already encountered several wing failures by the time they came to Barcelona. As Graham Hill went over the left-hand 'yump' for the ninth time, his rear wing supports buckled, then gave. With the down-force on the rear wheels suddenly reduced, the car went out of control, smashing into the guardrail and very nearly overturning.

Graham was happily unhurt, but soon noticed that his team-mate's wing was going the same way. Noticing the distortion, he sent a mechanic back to the Lotus pit, with the suggestion that Rindt be called in.

Before this could happen, however, Jochen also crashed, his car hurtling into Hill's wreckage and going upside down. The Englishman, still on the scene, helped in the rescue. Bloody and bruised, Rindt was fortunate to be alive.

In the midst of all this, Amon took over the lead, which he extended without difficulty. After 55 of the 90 laps the Ferrari headed Stewart's Matra by three-quarters of a minute, but then came the usual slice of Amon Luck. The Italian V12 seized, leaving Chris to walk sadly back to the pits.

During that '69 season, the New Zealander recalls, *I always used to put my cigarettes and lighter in the pocket of my overalls. Nine times out of ten, I knew I was going to have to park the thing miles from anywhere . . .*

So Stewart was left in the lead, after a thoroughly uncompetitive afternoon, and the Tyrrell-run MS80 finally won by two clear laps from Bruce McLaren.

We were just off the pace that day, recalls JYS, *but I had another worry as well, a fear, really. I'd seen Graham's shunt, but knew he was all right. Then, on another lap, I saw him beside his car, looking under it. Next thing, Jochen crashed in the same place, but I saw him moving in the cockpit, so I knew he was OK. What really scared me was the thought that he'd hit Graham's car while Graham was still looking underneath. And then I saw a marshal draw his finger across his throat. After that I was sure that Graham was dead. I can still remember the incredible relief I felt at the end of the race. The victory didn't really mean anything.*

Silverstone 1969

On the first morning of practice for the 1969 British Grand Prix Jochen Rindt was about at the end of his tether with Lotus. Few were in any doubt that here was the fastest driver in the world, but by mid-season he had not scored a single World Championship point. He had dominated in Spain, but crashed horrifically when his car's rear wing broke away, and at Zandvoort he had been leading easily until halted with a broken drive-shaft.

Serious also were the team's internal problems. Jochen was barely on speaking terms with Colin Chapman, and now, at Silverstone, he was fighting to keep himself under control. The Lotus boss was convinced that the future lay with his new four-wheel-drive 63,

but Rindt and team-mate Graham Hill had no enthusiasm for the project, preferring to stick with their 49s. Chapman, therefore, decided to solve the problem by selling two of the three 49s, retaining one for the team, along with a couple of 63s.

When Jochen heard of this apparent *fait accompli,* his response was swift: he would not drive the 63 – whose concept and design he did not trust – under any circumstances. For Silverstone, therefore, Chapman had to ask Jo Bonnier to loan back his car to the team, the Swede graciously accepting one of the dread 63s on a temporary basis. A similar car was assigned to John Miles, and the problems became so involved that, by the time of first practice for the British Grand Prix, the red, white and gold transporter had not arrived. While Rindt fumed, a similarly disgruntled Hill put in a few laps in a works Brabham, Jack himself having been hurt in a testing accident shortly before.

At lunchtime the cars arrived, and Jochen, after barely a word with Chapman, set third fastest time. The following day, at his magnificent best, the Austrian claimed pole position, a mite quicker than Jackie Stewart, whose own Matra had been damaged the day before and who was now in his team-mate's car.

These distinctly unpromising beginnings provided possibly the most exciting racing ever seen at Silverstone. Between Rindt and Stewart there was a deep friendship and an intense rivalry. Both trusted the other implicitly on the track, much as Jones and Villeneuve would do ten years later.

After a single lap it was obvious that this was a two-horse race, for Jochen and Jackie drifted out of Woodcote more than three seconds clear of the third man, Hulme. Sixty laps of pure Grand Prix magic were about to unfold. Sometimes the Matra and Lotus went through corners side by side, inches apart. Stewart took the lead after five laps, then Rindt took it back after ten more. The Scot has fond memories of the day.

It was fantastic, an intense battle, yet full of good humour. Occasionally we'd go through Becketts or somewhere, side by side, neither of us willing to give way, yet taking care always to give the other fellow room. And we'd come out of the corner, look across at each other! The problem was that scrapping away like that was time-consuming, so I decided to

Bruce McLaren on the grid

sit behind him for a while. That way we could leave the rest behind . . .

For most of the afternoon they continued like this, rarely more than a second apart. Was Stewart waiting to pounce? Or did Rindt have something in hand? It looked like being a sensational finish, but the crowd groaned in disbelief on lap 63 when the Matra came through alone. Rindt rushed into the pits. The left hand side plate of his rear wing had started to come away and was rubbing against the tyre. Quickly he rejoined, but Stewart was now half a minute ahead, and it was hopeless. With six laps left it became worse than that, for the Lotus came in again, this time stammering out of fuel. Jackie went on for an easy victory, and Jochen finished an inconsolable fourth.

All seemed to be over between Rindt and Chapman, but two weeks later, at the Nürburgring, the two men had a long talk and resolved their problems. Chapman had already made alternative arrangements for Hill for the 1970 season, and now feared that he would lose Jochen. If the Austrian would stay, he promised, the team would devote itself to making him World Champion. Which, of course, it did.

Denny Hulme

Graham Hill after a practice accident at Monaco

Brabham loses the Monaco GP at the last corner

Spa 1970

You know, I had some pretty frustrating days in motor racing, but that race at Spa must rank as the worst! Pedro hadn't been particularly quick in practice, although he was always good at Spa, and Jackie, Jochen and I were quite a bit ahead of him. Then comes race day – and he blows past us with no bother at all! The BRM V12 had us on acceleration out of the corners, and was also way quicker at the top end. After three or four laps it was pretty clearly a straight fight between the two of us, and I struggled to try and stay in the BRM's slipstream, just knowing that sooner or later it had to blow up. But that day, of course, it didn't . . .

For virtually the whole of the 1970 Belgian Grand Prix, Chris Amon's March 701 followed Pedro Rodriguez in the BRM P153, and the crowds were enthralled. Here, after all, were two drivers who went to Spa-Francorchamps in the right frame of mind, prepared to forget the inherent dangers of a sweeping road circuit

with a lap speed of 240 kmh (150 mph). Instead they savoured the satisfaction of driving round it as fast as they knew. It was good that they did, too, for Grand Prix cars never returned to the 14.1-kilometre (8.76-mile) track. Thereafter, Formula 1 and Belgium met only at the nonentities of Zolder and Nivelles.

Jackie Stewart, like Jimmy Clark before him, loathed Spa. Unlike Jimmy, he campaigned endlessly to have it removed from the World Championship, and in this he was ultimately successful. He went unwillingly to the 1970 race, full of misgivings and quite determined that this should be the last. It was typical of the man, however, that once in the racing car he put such thoughts out of his mind and applied himself to the task in hand. He was fastest in practice, followed by Rindt's Lotus 49 and Amon's March. Rodriguez was sixth with the BRM, a second and a half away.

At the end of the first lap Amon led from Stewart and Rindt, but Rodriguez was already up into fourth, which became second three laps later. At the end of lap five the BRM was in the lead, having passed Amon on the Masta straight. By now Chris had a lone fight on his hands, for Stewart and Rindt were already falling away with engine problems.

It was a pretty terrible feeling, recalls the New Zealander, when Pedro went by, because it was clear that the BRM had a lot more steam than my Cosworth. Aerodynamically the March was working quite well at Spa, but even so it was a real scratch to keep up. There was a lot of oil coming from the BRM, and I was sure it had to blow up. During the last half of the race I drove right at the limit – including making myself take the Masta kink flat – but Pedro drove beautifully that day. He made just one mistake, at La Source, and I got by him, but he took me again on acceleration past the pits.

On and on went the two cars, never more than three seconds apart and usually appreciably less. Their duel completely captured the crowd's attention, for there was little else of interest in the race. Jacky Ickx, their hero, had a troubled time with the Ferrari, but his team-mate Ignazio Giunti, making his Formula 1 debut, finished an impressive fourth.

Amon took the March round to a new lap record shortly before the end, but even this – an average of over 245 kmh (152 mph) – was not enough to take him past Rodriguez. At the finish Pedro was a fraction over one second ahead. For the last 14 of the 28 laps both men ran consistently under their fastest practice laps . . .

After the finish Rodriguez, not a hair out of place, calmly accepted the flowers and waved to the fans. Second, but exhilarated by the day, Amon grinned at him, lit the first of many post-race cigarettes.

I flew back to England soon after the race, and that night a bunch of us went out to a bistro in London. I remember sitting

there and thinking how unreal it all was. Had it really been that same afternoon that I'd run Spa at the limit? That was the thing about Spa . . . if you were satisfied with your driving there, it gave you a high for days. No other track did that. And I knew from Pedro's expression, as we shook hands afterwards, that he felt the same way . . .

Zandvoort 1970

An abiding memory of the 1970 Dutch Grand Prix is the sight of the winner on the podium afterwards. Jochen Rindt had dominated, and the Lotus 72 had come good. Before them, very obviously, stretched the World Championship. And there stood the Austrian, garland round his neck, tears in his eyes.

A few weeks before, Jochen had also won at Monaco after a drive which left onlookers aghast. There, too, he had wept in an outpouring of relief and joy and nervous exhaustion. At Zandvoort he was lamenting, in victory, the death of a friend.

Earlier in the year he had talked enthusiastically of

Colin Chapman's new car, but the revolutionary 72's first steps had been faltering ones and the team had fallen back on the immortal 49. For the Dutch Grand Prix, though, there was a revised car, with much of the sophistication removed. In this form, it immediately found favour with Jochen, and he had little difficulty in taking pole position. Next up were Jackie Stewart, making the best of his March 701, and Jacky Ickx, whose new flat-12 Ferrari 312B was starting to fulfil its promise.

The afternoon was overcast. Ickx made a tremendous start, blasting away into a lead which he kept for only a couple of laps. Going into Tarzan for the third time Rindt flicked out of the Ferrari's slipstream, and calmly outbraked it for the lead. Thereafter Jochen simply drove away, leaving Ickx to fend off Stewart. Making notable progress in his first Formula 1 drive was Clay Regazzoni, running sixth with his Ferrari. He would finish fourth.

After 23 laps there were gaps in everyone's charts: Piers Courage and Jo Siffert were missing, and suddenly we became aware of a huge cloud of black smoke wafting into the grey sky. Clearly there had been an enormous accident on the far side of the circuit. After

a few minutes the commentator announced, erroneously, that Courage and Siffert had crashed together, adding, unforgivably, that both men were unhurt. Siffert had not been involved in any accident, but had stopped with engine failure. In the paddock his wife and friends celebrated his escape.

And so the race went on, Rindt from Ickx from Stewart from Regazzoni. With 30 laps to go, the Belgian Ferrari driver came in with a puncture, which dropped him to fourth. Quickly he repassed his teammate, but there was no question of further progress. The last few laps seemed interminable. Not until then, fully an hour after the accident, did the commentator stumblingly admit that there had been a mistake, that 'Piers Courage died in his car.'

A ghastly afternoon, then, with more grief for this curious band of travellers. Frank Williams, whose de Tomaso Courage had been driving, was left stunned by the tragedy. With the death of Bruce McLaren in the very recent past, this new disaster was almost more than people could take in. The afternoon had provided a clear pointer to the rest of the season: Lotus versus Ferrari. At the time, though, such a thing was not of immediate importance.

Monza 1970

This was a weekend of Grand Prix racing *in extremis*. Chicane blight had not yet attacked with any virulence, and Monza was still a wide-open 'honest-to-God' *blast!* The lap speed was around 240 kmh (150 mph), yet there were corners – notably the Lesmos – which were a true test of ability. For the Lesmos you needed to balance your ability with judgement, confidence and courage, and the same was true of the Curva Grande.

Monza has a special feel about it. Apart from being breathlessly quick, it is imbued with tradition, marinated in more than half a century of racing folklore, a place of passion. Many drivers dislike it, but none can be unmoved by its sinister grandeur.

Jochen, non ti dimenticare. That, more than anything else, was what I remember of Sunday, 6 September 1970. I was driving – a few feet at a time – past the Hotel de Ville in Monza on my way to the track, and I saw the words daubed on the rear window of a Fiat 500. One man's clumsy, yet immensely touching, tribute to a great driver lost. And there were others, too, wherever you looked. There were photographs of him, bordered by black sticky tape, on the countless coaches bringing *tifosi* to Monza from all over the country.

Jochen Rindt, the World Champion elect, had died the afternoon before, when his Lotus had gone out of control under braking for the Parabolica. It could not have been driver error which caused the car to pitch into the barrier. The Austrian, with dreadful injuries to his throat from the safety belt buckle, died very soon after the accident.

Italians *feel* their motor racing. Rindt was an Austrian in a British car, and he died in a place where, by tradition, only Ferrari counts for anything. For all that, the sense of grief that morning was overpowering. A hero was gone, a man who had driven with his heart.

The atmosphere, therefore, was already heavily charged when the cars were wheeled out. There was a Ferrari on each of the first three rows: Jacky Ickx, Clay Regazzoni, Ignazio Giunti. From the start the red trio was heavily involved, and the partisans confidently expected a home victory. But they fell a little silent after half an hour or so. Giunti and Ickx were out. Only Regazzoni remained to fight the good fight. The Swiss was going well, but this was only his fifth Grand Prix, and he had a reputation for making mistakes under

Peterson, Siffert and Ickx come out of Casino Square, 1971 Monaco GP

Michael Turner '71

pressure. And this day pressure he certainly had – from Stewart, Beltoise, Hulme and Stommelen.

Clay made his move with a dozen laps left, increasing the pace, gradually going clear, weaving dramatically past the pits to shake the rest out of his slipstream. Behind, Beltoise momentarily delayed Stewart, and it was done. The tow was lost, and Gianclaudio had only to stay on the road for victory.

The wall of sound from Monza's dusty old concrete grandstand built steadily as the Ferrari went round for the last time, erupting as a crescendo when Regazzoni emerged from Parabolica. He swept over the line a new and instant national hero, and the fans clambered over the fence in their thousands. By the time Cevert arrived, in sixth place, the road was swamped. François had to brake the March hard and thread his way through to the flag.

After an endless wait the Ferrari reappeared at the end of its slowing down lap. Almost before it had stopped, Clay had been plucked from the cockpit, hoisted onto shoulder and carried to the rostrum. 'Reg-a-zzon-i-reg-a-zzon-i', went the chant. In the anarchy of the moment a man was shoved against the 312B's exhausts and badly burned. He, more than most, would remember the 41st Italian Grand Prix.

Monaco 1971

At Monaco in 1971 there was unseasonal weather on the Côte d'Azur. The first day of practice was marked by a deluge which never let up, and the tortured shriek of Chris Amon's Matra, easily fastest, resounded round the circuit as it sought grip on the streaming track. Mario Andretti, new to the joys of Monaco, clearly thought it all a little strange.

At the traditional early morning practice session on Friday, the track surface was still damp in places, but Jackie Stewart's Tyrrell was a clear second faster than the rest, and pole position was settled. Next up were Ickx (Ferrari), Siffert (BRM), Amon, Rodriguez (BRM), Hulme (McLaren), Beltoise (Matra) and Peterson (March).

On Saturday there was more rain, finer but enough to keep Andretti from the race. His car had broken during the only dry session, and his efforts to set a qualifying time in the wet were something to see. Fastest this time was Peterson. This was Ronnie's second season of Formula 1, and he was really beginning to make his name. The year before, spent driving a privately-entered March 701, had been unremarkable. Now in the works team, he was at the wheel of the 711, a hideous but effective racing machine.

Only eighth on the grid, Peterson faced a difficult task in the race, for overtaking at Monaco – even on the old circuit, used in 1971 for the last time – was never easy. But he and several others received a lucky break shortly before the start. Amon – who else? – lost his fuel pressure on the grid, and the Matra was quickly pushed to the side of the road. Pedro Rodriguez, never one to miss an opportunity, quickly slotted his BRM into the vacant space, which left a gap in front of Ronnie.

He made the most of it, too, jinking to the right of Hulme and beating the McLaren into Ste Devote. At the end of the first lap it was Stewart, Siffert, Ickx, Rodriguez and Peterson.

Right from the start Ronnie was looking to get past Pedro, but the Mexican could be extremely obstructive on occasions, and this was one of them. Peterson took a lunge at the BRM on lap seven, but was shut out so violently that he locked his brakes and was overtaken by Hulme.

A little angry now, Ronnie quickly repassed the McLaren, then set about Rodriguez once more, passing him into the Gasworks hairpin on lap 13. By now the leading trio was well clear, but Peterson set his course and started to catch Ickx. On lap 30 he passed him. It was inspired, without a doubt, and the crowd looked on in astonishment as, just one lap later, he outbraked Siffert for second place!

Could he catch Stewart? Surely not, for the Tyrrell was 17 seconds ahead now. But, being Ronnie Peterson, he tried. Jackie had everything well in hand, and set a stunning new lap record to keep the young man in check. But Ronnie never relaxed his pace, never allowed Stewart the luxury of taking it easy. Nearly all his race laps were quicker than he had managed in practice, and those who had witnessed Jochen Rindt's drive the previous year suddenly had a new hero. It was unforgettable.

Barcelona 1971

Psychologically, that win at Barcelona in '71 did me a lot of good. I'd been without a win for a full year – since the previous Spanish Grand Prix, in fact – and the sport had been through a lot of tragedy in the meantime. We'd lost Jochen and Bruce and Piers, and I think my enthusiasm was at a pretty low ebb, despite the fact that, in the Tyrrell, I obviously had a much more competitive car than I'd had the year before. I'd been through twelve pretty miserable months, *so therefore, when I had that victory at Barcelona it lifted me a lot.*

Jackie Stewart was at his wonderful best in Spain that day. He had won the inaugural race at the majestic Montjuich Park two years before, but that came to him through luck, a fact he readily admitted. In 1971 he won because he drove the race better than anyone else. It was as straightforward as that.

At that time people were already suggesting that the Cosworth engine had seen its best days, that the 12-cylinder era was nigh. Ferrari had closed the previous season with an almost unbroken series of victories, and at this early point in the new season were still running the same elegant 312B cars. At Barcelona Jacky Ickx took pole position in one of them, with team-mate Clay Regazzoni next to him and the Matra of Chris Amon making up the front row. The first of the Cosworth cars was Stewart's Tyrrell, fourth fastest in practice.

To avoid any clash with bullfights elsewhere in the city, the organisers decided on an early start. At midday, with the heat at its fiercest, they were on their way. Ickx made a great start to lead Regazzoni and Stewart into the first hairpin, but the Scot was soon past Clay and moving in on the leading Ferrari.

I knew it was vital to get in front as soon as possible, try and build up a lead while the Ferraris were heavy with fuel. I was sure that Ickx would be much more dangerous in the second half of the race . . .

To that end Stewart pressured the Belgian driver very hard. At the end of lap five Ickx made a slight mistake at the last uphill corner before the pits, allowing his rival to take a run at the lead. Stewart actually passed the Ferrari at the 240 kmh (150 mph) brow before the plunge down to the hairpin, slicing through a gap between Ickx and the Armco barrier that must have been all of a foot wider than the Tyrrell. It was a beautiful and incisive move, and assured Stewart of the line into the hairpin. That done, he was gone.

In the early stages it seemed that a possible challenge to Stewart might come from Amon, for the New Zealander quickly disposed of Regazzoni and closed right up to Ickx – whereupon the Matra broke a rear shock absorber. Chris kept going to the end, finishing third, but he was never a serious threat.

The race belonged completely to the leading pair, and Stewart's theory about a late challenge from Ickx proved entirely correct. After 50 of the 75 laps the Tyrrell led by almost 10 seconds, but thereafter the Ferrari began to pare down the gap. With 10 laps left

Ickx was within three seconds of Stewart, and both men were lapping faster than they had managed in qualifying. It was truly heroic stuff from two great drivers, but Stewart was not about to be caught, passing the chequered flag three and a half seconds to the good. The Tyrrell had won its first race, and JYS was beginning a sequence of success which would lead to his second World Championship.

Zandvoort 1971

A memorable battle, this one, between the two best wet-weather drivers of their time. Jacky Ickx and Pedro Rodriguez qualified first and second, their times set in the first – and only – completely dry practice session.

Joining them on the front row was Jackie Stewart, another brilliant rain driver, so the persistent drizzle on race morning suggested a three-way fight.

Not so. Ickx-Rodriguez-Stewart was the order at the

Nanni Galli in a March (18) and François Cevert in a Tyrrell come together in the 1971 Dutch Grand Prix

end of the first lap, and the story was the same as they completed lap two, but the Tyrrell was already nine seconds behind the Ferrari and the BRM, and Jackie was clearly not going to play a significant role in this race. At the end of lap three, he was back in eighth . . .

The Dutch Grand Prix of 1971 was a straightforward duel, in which tyres played a crucial part. What you needed that day was a set of Firestones. If you were on Goodyears, like Stewart, Amon and Beltoise, you merely circulated.

In many ways, the race was something apart from the rest of the 1971 season. Ferrari, for example, were going through dreadful times with their 312B2, essentially a clumsy and far less predictable 'development' of the highly successful 312B of the year before. It was the first year of slick tyres, and, on the Ferrari chassis, Firestones set up such a vibration through the car that the drivers complained of double vision through really quick corners.

If Firestone lagged a little during the early days of the slick, however, they had a clear advantage in the rain.

Equally, a poor chassis mattered less on a slippery track, where throttle control was at a premium. Here, Ickx and Rodriguez were supreme.

Jacky led the early going, but a few laps into the race the rain came down more strongly, and Pedro pounced, neatly outbraking the Ferrari into Tarzan. In the torrential conditions the Mexican pulled out the lead to as much as eight seconds, but as the rain abated once more, Ickx began to close in again. On lap 30 he led. Next time round it was Rodriguez, then Ickx again, and there the Belgian stayed for the rest of the race..

Pedro, typically, never lost heart, but in the treacherous conditions he had a difficult time with the BRM, which refused to run properly at low revs. As a consequence, the driver had often to use a lower gear than he would have wished, and this gave him tremendous wheelspin problems out of the slow corners. His was clearly a more arduous task, yet the pressure on Ickx never relented. At the chequered flag, the Ferrari was less than eight seconds ahead. It had been two hours of pure inspiration from the leading pair.

Well, said Jacky on the podium, *today I am happy to win without problem* . . . and then he flashed a broad smile at Pedro.

For everyone else, it was a complete rout. Clay Regazzoni took a gallant and lonely third place, his Ferrari without its nosecone for the last few laps, but even the Swiss was lapped. And Stewart? He was 11th, five laps behind the winner, having spent much of his afternoon in company with the March (Firestone-shod, of course) of Alex Soler-Roig . . .

In the traffic afterwards, Pedro sat patiently in his Porsche 911, replete with trademarks, deerstalker and sun glasses. Disappointed, yes, but in his expression there was a deep satisfaction at a courageous job well done. It was the last great day of his racing career. Three weeks later, at the Norisring, he lost his life in an unimportant sports car race.

Watkins Glen 1971

In 1971 Watkins Glen was still the town of plenty for Grand Prix racing. The era of standardisation was some way off. Quirks were tolerated, and practice sessions scheduled according to the whim of the organiser. Bernie Ecclestone had not yet bought the Brabham team, let alone formed the Formula One Constructors Association. Some races paid a great deal more than others, and Watkins Glen was the plum.

The sport's governing body – known at that time as the CSI – maintained a dozy vigil in Paris, a few blazered old sportsmen with a penchant for leather armbands. There were no rules about nominating drivers before the start of a season, or anything of that kind. If a team cared to enter a third car occasionally, or even a fourth, that was just fine.

For the Glen, where pickings were unusually rich, there were three Tyrrells in 1971, with Peter Revson joining the regular pairing of Jackie Stewart and François Cevert. Start money apart, the American's appearance was a fruitless exercise, for he qualified

poorly and retired after a single lap with a broken clutch.

Watkins Glen in October invariably meant freezing conditions. Occasionally there was heavy rain, sometimes fog. In the early morning of race day in 1971, there was both, but by 10 o'clock a god somewhere had clicked his fingers, the sky was cloudless blue, the temperature in the seventies. The crowd was the largest in the Glen's history.

For that year of 1971 there were major changes at Watkins Glen, a new loop of a little over a mile adding 40 seconds to the lap time. The paddock was still unpaved and primitive, but there was new, pale blue, armco barrier bordering the entire length of the track on both sides. With a massive attendance and a winner's purse of $50,000, everything seemed very secure.

The race went to Tyrrell, as most had predicted, for 1971 was a year in which Jackie Stewart was usually unassailable. He had clinched his second World Championship as early as August, and his pole position at the

Glen was his sixth of the year. But he did not win. After leading from the start in accustomed fashion, the Scot quickly began to suffer tyre problems. With only 12 laps gone, the Tyrrell was understeering savagely, and Cevert, right behind his idol, was becoming embarrassed. Jacky Ickx's Ferrari ran a threatening third. What should François do?

Stewart quickly solved his young team-mate's problem, however, by waving him through, and then working strenuously to hold off the rest, allowing Cevert to build a cushion. The only real threat came from Ickx, who that day drove one of his greatest races, keeping the pressure on, running between two and four seconds off the lead. Ten laps from the end, the question was resolved when the Ferrari's alternator began to fall off, leaving Cevert home free. The gallant Stewart finished fifth.

It is always pleasurable to witness a first Grand Prix win because a racing driver's face is never so honestly joyful again. It is something beyond mere championship points and a hefty cheque. That comes later. François Cevert's gipsy eyes shone with rapture as he stood, both arms raised, on the victory rostrum, an enormous garland round his neck.

Two years on, in 1973, the Tyrrell team was back, with three cars, for Stewart, Cevert and Chris Amon. By now François was virtually as quick as Jackie, and it was clear that the Frenchman would lead the team in 1974. Watkins Glen would be Stewart's 100th Grand Prix. The World Championship was already clinched, and rumours of his impending retirement gathered strength.

In the course of the Saturday morning practice session Cevert proved the quickest Tyrrell driver. Towards the end of it, he went out again and crashed at the ultra-fast Esses. It was an accident of extraordinary violence, and François was killed instantly. Later, Ken sorrowfully withdrew his other cars.

Ken Tyrrell and François Cevert

Monaco 1972

The Monaco Grand Prix of 1972 was a most curious event. This was the last race through the Principality before the circuit's classic layout was changed, before the desire to instal more grandstand seats – and to extract more francs – resulted in that absurd loop around the swimming pool, which made Monte Carlo for all time a no-overtaking zone.

In 1972, though, that wonderful curving drag down to the old Gasworks Hairpin was still in play. But there was a change in the track, the famous chicane being moved down the road to a point immediately before Tabac. A year later it reverted to its original position.

There were other changes, too. For once, and once only, 25 cars were allowed to start on the tiny circuit – this after a row which delayed the start of practice. The weather was anything but Riviera delight, and Saturday afternoon was marred by a cloudburst. The grid was curious too, in that Jackie Stewart, hitherto almost unbeatable at Monte Carlo, was down in eighth place. There was something wrong: Stewart was unknowingly suffering the consequences of an ulcer, which would later keep him out of racing for six weeks.

On race day the weather was appalling, with rain lashing down from mid-day on, and a strong biting wind swirling in from the sea. Fittipaldi's Lotus and Ickx's Ferrari made up the front row, with Regazzoni and Beltoise next up, then Amon and Gethin, Hulme and Stewart.

Conditions at the start were truly dreadful, and all the logical money was on Ickx, brilliant in the wet, starting from the front and with 12-cylinder smoothness and torque working with him. But there was a wild card. Jean-Pierre Beltoise was about to have his greatest day.

I knew, he relates now, *that everything would depend on the start. That's normal in any wet race – because only the leader can see! But no one on the grid that day had ever raced at Monaco in the rain, I knew that, and it was clear to me that passing would be impossible because of the lack of space and visibility. The man in front, I was sure, would be able to break away, and therefore I decided to risk everything to lead before the first corner . . .*

The ploy worked. Jean-Pierre had the BRM alongside Ickx's Ferrari into Ste Devote. The car twitched under braking, but just made it through.

Capitalising on his clear vision, Beltoise drove an inspired first lap, the red and white car slithering down to Gasworks before the others had emerged from Tabac. Jean-Pierre was a little staggered by his lead: *I could see no one in my mirrors, and prepared myself for a red flag . . .*

Most people made mistakes that afternoon, including Stewart who spun while catching Ickx. Beltoise himself had many a 'sweaty-palm' moment – including a half-spin at Portiers – when lapping others, sometimes indiscreetly. But Jean-Pierre was meant to win that day. Somehow he avoided hitting anything. Ickx's challenge was gallantly untiring, but fruitless. At the end of 80 very long laps, the Ferrari was more than half a minute adrift.

Beltoise was tearful as he talked with the Rainiers afterwards, an outflow of emotion and relief. It was his first Grand Prix victory, and he had driven brilliantly. But he never won another – and neither did BRM.

Clermont-Ferrand 1972

In the course of nine years as a Grand Prix driver, Jackie Stewart won 27 Grands Prix – more than any driver in history – and very few came his way through luck. Usually his victories were won by a blend of intelligence and sheer superiority.

It was not so at Clermont-Ferrand in 1972. Stewart's hectic existence had caught up with him a few weeks before. After a lack-lustre Monaco Grand Prix, he had undergone tests which revealed the presence of a bleeding duodenal ulcer. That being the case, he missed the Belgian Grand Prix, but felt fit enough to return for the French.

Jackie, like many drivers, had mixed feelings about Clermont-Ferrand, on the one hand glorying in the sheer magnificence of the mountain circuit, on the other worrying about its narrowness and somewhat primitive safety facilities. He qualified his Tyrrell third and reported that he felt very much better.

New Tyrrell at Clermont-Ferrand in 1972, used by both drivers in practice but not raced

Race day brought huge queues on the winding roads from the town up to the track. The weather was perfect, and on pole position was the only French car in the race: the new Matra MS120D, driven by Chris Amon. After practice the New Zealander truly felt that at last he was going to win a Grand Prix.

That was also how it looked when they were flagged away, Amon immediately taking the lead, shadowed by Denny Hulme's McLaren and, of course, Stewart. For the best part of an hour the trio ran together, with Amon very calm and confident in the lead, stretching the Matra no more than he needed . . .

Eventually he had to stretch it to the full. After 19 of the 38 laps, Chris headed for the pits. The Matra had a puncture, just as Hulme's McLaren had suffered a few laps earlier. And there was Jackie Stewart to scoop it all up.

When Amon resumed, he was in eighth place, more than a minute behind the Tyrrell, and there began one of the greatest drives of modern times. It was a day when every other driver on the track looked pedestrian.

Angry and frustrated, Chris overtook the likes of Hailwood, Cevert and Peterson, shattering the lap record time and again.

I never saw anything special about that drive, he later said. *I was going pretty well, sure, but the main thing was that, for once, the Matra was going well. It was a track where sheer horsepower didn't count for too much . . .* By the end, Amon and the MS120D were third, having taken more than half a minute from Stewart's lead.

And the Scot's comments afterwards? *Well, the thing about Clermont is the stones. People put wheels off the road and shower the track with stones. I was driving carefully the whole time, concentrating on keeping away from them, not putting a wheel off . . .* It was a piece of magnificent Stewart one-upmanship – and it fooled no one. At Clermont you could not *avoid* the stones, for others peppered the road with them. All you could do was hope that your tyres would survive. And if you had luck to match your skill, as Jackie always did, you quietly put it down to superior judgement, keeping the legend intact . . .

Brands Hatch 1972

Emerson Fittipaldi was on something of a streak when the Grand Prix circus arrived at Brands Hatch for the British Grand Prix of 1972. He had won in the black Lotus 72 at Jarama and Nivelles, and high placings elsewhere had contributed to a sizeable lead in the World Championship. Earlier in the year he had won the Race of Champions at Brands, and the chances of a repeat were excellent. The momentum of the season was with him.

In practice, however, no one had any answer to Jacky Ickx, who put the Ferrari 312B2 on pole position, followed by Fittipaldi, Stewart (Tyrrell) and Revson (McLaren). After his stunning drive at Clermont-Ferrand a fortnight earlier, Chris Amon had high hopes of the new Matra MS120D, but he damaged it during qualifying and had to revert to the older car, effectively putting himself out of the reckoning.

On paper, then, it was a three-car race: Ickx, Fittipaldi and Stewart. As ever Brands was lucky with the weather, the day so unexpectedly hot that the track surface began to break up.

Ickx made a sensational start, getting the fuel-heavy Ferrari into Paddock ahead of Fittipaldi, while Beltoise nosed his BRM into third place. In the early laps, indeed, the Frenchman was something of a menace, clearly holding up those immediately behind, one of whom was a frustrated Stewart. After seven laps, though, Jackie had the Tyrrell past and away, driving really hard to catch the two leaders.

After 20 laps the Ferrari and the Lotus were still running together, with Emerson not looking like going by. Jacky was driving the cumbersome red car beautifully, setting an impressive pace, with Stewart apparently unable to close.

JYS got his chance, however, when the lapping began. Both Ickx and Fittipaldi were held up, and the Tyrrell was instantly with them. Now all three were running at the limit, and Emerson was the first to make a mistake, missing his braking point at Druids and skating wide on the crumbling track. That put Stewart up into second place, but he could not get onto terms with Ickx.

Shortly before half-distance the trio came upon Wilson Fittipaldi's Brabham, again at the approach to Druids. And, keen to assert his loyalty to 'The Family',

Wilson made sure that Stewart was held up, and Emerson was second once more.

On and on went the Ferrari, but both his pursuers had noticed wisps of oily smoke from the back of the car, had reasoned that engines need lubrication and had decided to let nature take its course. An oil cooler union had loosened, and on lap 49 Ickx saw the needle on his pressure gauge take a final dive. A great drive was over, and now it was Stewart versus Fittipaldi to the flag.

Although the Tyrrell was frequently within a second of the Lotus, it was apparent that Stewart was having a much harder time than his rival, whose car was far more at ease over the appalling bumps of Brands Hatch. In the closing laps, indeed, Emerson extended his advantage, and was four seconds to the good at the flag. Further victories at the Osterreichring and Monza that year saw him to the title. It was a brilliant season, and Fittipaldi never showed the same out-and-out competitiveness again, thereafter substituting stealth and canniness for raw aggression.

Nürburgring 1972

To be honest with you, that victory was one of the easiest I ever had – much more straightforward than I expected. I started from pole position, yes, but by less than two seconds; and two seconds over more than 14 miles is nothing at all. I expected a fight from Stewart and Fittipaldi, but it never happened. You know, you have very few races in your life where everything is perfect, but this was one . . .

As was very often the case, Jacky Ickx underestimated his performance when recalling the 1972 German Grand Prix. From the start of his career in Formula 1, the Belgian had been one of those very few who actually conquer the Nürburgring, by confronting it squarely, without trepidation. To do that, you need absolute faith in self and car. Ickx never doubted his own ability – at the 'Ring or anywhere else – and he knew that the Ferrari would stay in one piece. Oh, it might blow up or break its gearbox, something to bring it to a halt. It would not, however, snap its suspension, start shedding wheels on the plunge down to Adenau or Pflanzgarten, and that kind of mental security can count for a lot. Racing cars crash, after all, either because something within them breaks or because their drivers give them the wrong command. Jacky Ickx had faith in himself and the car. Thus equipped, he felt, there was nothing to fear.

For all that, his performance was great. By mid-season of 1972, Ferrari had got their B2 chassis to handle with reasonable precision, but it was in no sense the equal of those from Lotus, Tyrrell or March. It had strength, of course, and that very remarkable flat-12 engine. Most of all, at the Nürburgring, it had Ickx. In practice Jacky lapped in 7 minutes 7.0 seconds, and that gave him the pole. Next up were Stewart's Tyrrell, Fittipaldi's Lotus and Peterson's March. Regazzoni's Ferrari was back on the fourth row.

The Ferrari got away superbly, led into the South Curve and thereafter receded into the middle distance. At the end of the first lap Ickx led Peterson by more than three seconds, and it looked as though there was never the remotest chance that he would be seriously disturbed. Through the afternoon Jacky majestically pulled away, and at the flag was almost 50 seconds clear of the rest.

Behind him was the action. Stewart had made a very poor start, and ran only fifth for more than half the race. That became fourth when Fittipaldi's Lotus retired in a dramatic welter of flame, its shattered gearbox spewing oil onto hot exhausts. And then Jackie, along with Clay Regazzoni, got past Peterson.

For 50 miles the Tyrrell shadowed the Ferrari, and on the last lap Stewart thought he saw a way past Regga. Out of Hatzenbach the Swiss went a little wide, and into the next corner blue and red were side by side. The Ferrari emerged from it alone . . .

In the pits, a while later, Jackie held an angry, impromptu, press conference, giving vent to his feelings about Regazzoni. And Clay, with that inimitable air of injured innocence, said that Stewart had tried to pass 'in an impossible place.'

Ickx, however, was beyond all this. Up on the rostrum, a vast garland around his neck, he waved happily to the crowds after his first Grand Prix win in more than a year. He had crushed everyone with a perfect drive around this most daunting of circuits. Having never got along particularly well with his Scottish near-namesake, he will have found the last lap incident icing on a splendid cake. It was the last he was ever to taste after a Grand Prix.

Ickx and Peterson at the Adenau Bridge, 1972 German Grand Prix

Anderstorp 1973

This was a heart-breaker for Ronnie Peterson. For the first time Sweden had a World Championship Grand Prix, and Ronnie was the pace man throughout. Fastest in practice, he led away and seemed set for his first Formula 1 victory – and in front of his own people.

At this stage of his career Peterson was an intensely frustrated man. Generally acknowledged to be the out-and-out fastest of all the Grand Prix drivers, he had joined Lotus at the beginning of 1973 after three mixed seasons with March. His position in the scheme of things was directly comparable with that of Jochen Rindt four years earlier. Both had shown themselves to be virtually unbeatable in Formula 2, and neither had any difficulty in adapting their abilities to Formula 1. Both joined Lotus, as team-mate to a reigning World Champion, and both instantly proved themselves

quicker. But winning . . . that was something else again.

The race at Anderstorp was typical of Ronnie's fortunes during the first half of the 1973 season. He took pole position, followed by the Tyrrells of François Cevert and Jackie Stewart, the sister Lotus 72 of Emerson Fittipaldi, the Brabham BT42 of Carlos Reutemann and the McLaren M23 of Denny Hulme. And he took the lead immediately, with Fittipaldi slotting in behind him. The early laps, indeed, seemed to point to a conclusive Lotus day, for Cevert and Stewart, although they stayed with the black cars, did not look like getting by them.

This may have been the greatest race that Denny Hulme ever drove. From the beginning he had the McLaren at the tail of the five-car queue, but he fell

Peterson, Fittipaldi, Cevert, Stewart and Hulme, 1973 Swedish Grand Prix

away as the halfway point approached. He had come upon Oliver's Shadow and was preparing to lap it when Jack thoughtfully put two wheels in the sand, which showered the New Zealander's car and jammed its throttle slides.

Denny headed for the pits, but as he did so the engine died. Quickly he dropped the clutch and prodded the throttle to restart it – and that cleared the slides! Denis Clive Hulme grunted to himself, found a low gear and switched off his rev limiter. By now he had lost 15 seconds to the leaders, but was beginning a stunning drive.

At the front Peterson, Fittipaldi, Stewart and Cevert were still running in line astern, and as they went into their closing laps Jackie seemed ready to make a move, beginning to pressure Emerson very hard. With 10 laps left, the Brazilian's brakes were at the end of their tether, and he had no alternative but to let the Tyrrell through. By this time, astonishingly, Hulme was up with the pack and he followed Stewart by. With 10 laps to go the Lotus, Tyrrell and McLaren were tied together.

Now it was Stewart's turn for trouble, for his brakes failed completely, to the point that he needed the gearbox to slow for corners. Instantly Denny took second place, and the spectators groaned. Three laps to go! Surely Ronnie could not lose now?

Peterson's problem was a puncture in his nearside rear tyre, and he could not hold off Hulme, who duly overtook to win by four seconds. As ever Ronnie smiled in defeat, but it was a resigned smile. He had so much wanted this race, but he could have done nothing more.

Two weeks later, at Paul Ricard, there was another multi-car fight for the lead. Peterson was in there, of course, but his drive was strangely muted, lacking its usual aggression. Jody Scheckter led most of the way in a McLaren, but it was Fittipaldi who led the Lotus attack, with Ronne sitting behind them. This time the cards fell for him. Emerson took Jody and himself out of the race, and Peterson went on to win. Knowing the secret now, he then triumphed at the Osterreichring, Monza and Watkins Glen. Ronnie and the 72 . . . who can ever forget them?

Silverstone 1973

A classic race, from first to last. This was the last British Grand Prix to be run at Silverstone before the chicane was installed at Woodcote. There were perhaps sound reasons for its introduction, notably the safety of the spectators, but there is no getting away from the fact that it destroyed one of the most electrifying sights in Grand Prix racing. You could stand on the outside of Woodcote and watch a really great driver teeter through, showing the art of Grand Prix driving to its full. Here a blend of precision and courage made for something memorable.

Inevitably a chicane would have to be built at Woodcote, but perhaps an incident in the 1973 British Grand Prix brought it forward. It occurred at the end of the first lap . . .

Fresh from his victory at Paul Ricard a couple of weeks earlier, Ronnie Peterson was most people's favourite to win again at Silverstone, and in practice he duly took pole position with the Lotus 72, sharing the front row with the McLarens of Denny Hulme and Peter Revson. In row two were Jackie Stewart in a Tyrrell and Emerson Fittipaldi in a Lotus. Heading row

three was the third McLaren, driven by Jody Scheckter. In the French Grand Prix the South African – in only his third Grand Prix – had driven a sensational race, leading in spectacular style for most of the way before being bundled off the road by Fittipaldi. On the strength of this McLaren decided to run him at Silverstone.

As expected, Ronnie took the lead at the start, but it lasted only as far as Becketts. The Lotus had Stewart's Tyrrell on its tail, at the entry, but Jackie momentarily appeared not to brake for the corner, shooting by on the inside in a moment of quite extraordinary judgement. That Stewart was capable of such a manoeuvre so early in a race was incredible, and Ronnie shook his head in resignation as he came out of the corner. Jackie, it appeared, was going to walk away with this one, and he arrived at Woodcote with a sizeable lead.

Peterson and Reutemann followed the Tyrrell through, and then the chaos began. Scheckter, waved past by team-mate Hulme on the approach to Woodcote, began to run wide, the McLaren snapping into a spin as it came off the corner. At 240 kmh (150 mph) it slid across the road – in front of the pack – and hit the pit wall. In an instant there were fearful scenes with cars spinning everywhere, some becoming airborne. When everything settled, marshals discovered to their astonishment that only one driver, Andrea de Adamich, was hurt, and he not seriously. Out for the afternoon were Scheckter, Williamson, Follmer, Beltoise and the entire Surtees team of Pace, Mass and Hailwood.

The folly of exhibiting a red flag (to stop the race) only in the start-finish area was never more clearly demonstrated, for soon the leaders were back, and running at full speed. It was fortunate indeed that a man of Stewart's experience and skill was at their head, but the Scot had to work hard to bring his Tyrrell and the rest of the pack to a halt. An hour later the race was restarted.

This time Peterson again led from the start, but Stewart did not get away so well, and was soon out of the picture with gear selection problems. The race settled down into a four-car battle between Peterson, Hulme, Revson and the Hesketh-entered March of James Hunt. In the closing laps the American McLaren driver made a break and pulled away a little, leaving Peterson to fight both oversteer and Hulme. Revson finally won by a little under three seconds.

That really was an incredible race, recalls James Hunt. It was the first Grand Prix in which I was truly competitive, and it sticks in my mind for that reason. I was happy to be fourth, but I could probably have been second had my left front tyre not blistered badly in the last third of the race. I kept close to Ronnie and Denny right to the end in the hope that they might take each other off. They were obviously going to fight right to the line, but the nearest they came to a mistake was when Ronnie got sideways on the grass – right after taking the flag! The battle took all three of us closer to Revson again, but I think he always had the situation well under control . . .

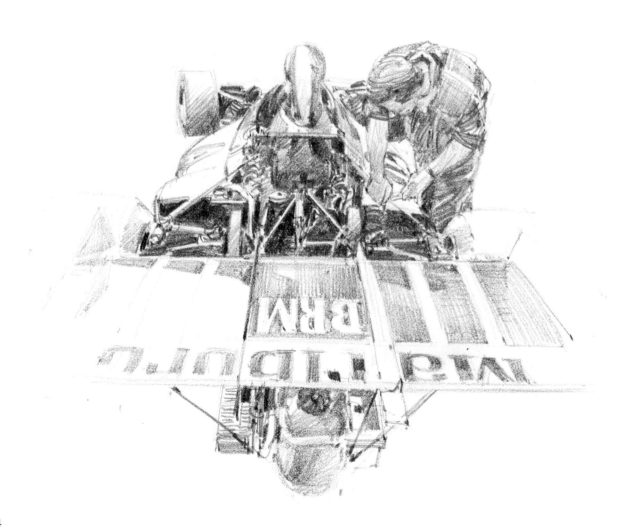

Revson wins 1973 British Grand Prix, followed by Peterson, Hulme and Hunt

Nürburgring 1973

There was always a special significance to victory at the Nürburgring, a fact admitted even by the most pragmatic of men. True, it brought only nine points, no more than Zolder or Paul Ricard, but its effect on a man's standing put it into another league. By the beginning of the 1970s, it was a race on its own, a link with tradition, fugitive from virtually every other Grand Prix on the calendar. Constantly there were murmurs of discontent about the circuit's inherent safety problems, but victory at the 'Ring remained the one most coveted by the drivers. The winner here followed in the tradition of Nuvolari, Caracciola, Rosemeyer, Ascari, Fangio, Moss and Clark. Even those ignorant of the sport's history felt themselves in the grip of the Nürburgring, where only the greatest excelled.

In early August of 1973, Jackie Stewart knew that this would be his final race at the 'Ring. A week earlier he had led François Cevert to a Tyrrell 1-2 in the Dutch Grand Prix, and was on course for his third World Championship. Already he had secretly committed himself to retirement at the end of the year.

If Stewart had a serious rival in Germany, it had to be Jacky Ickx. Honours were divided, each man having won twice in the last four races at the Nürburgring, but this year the Belgian, dominant in 1972, was in trouble. Ferrari were in the midst of a catastrophic season, and had temporarily withdrawn. A Grand Prix at the 'Ring without Ickx was inconceivable, and McLaren lost no time in making a third M23 available to him.

Stewart and Ickx were never the best of friends, having in common only a superlative ability to drive racing cars, and everyone looked forward with relish to a keen confrontation in Germany.

Jacky took to his new car immediately, being the first man in practice to set a really quick time. But he lost half the session with a blown engine, in which time Stewart, Peterson and Cevert all went a little quicker – although none equalled Ickx's pole time of the previous year.

The final day was marred by showers, which meant that the 22.5-kilometre (14-mile) track was never dry in its entirety. Despite that, however, Jacky all but equalled his time of the day before, and was more than six seconds quicker than the next man . . . Stewart!

It was hot and dry once more on race day, but sadly the great confrontation never came to be. McLaren opted for hard tyres, and after a single lap it was obvious that Ickx would not stay with the Tyrrells. His car ran perfectly throughout, but so also did the two blue ones ahead of him. Later he described it as the most frustrating race of his life. At the flag he was 40 seconds behind.

For the second time in a week Stewart and Cevert achieved a perfect result, and there was something mesmeric about the progress of the cars as they swirled round in perfect formation, as if guided by a divine hand. It was the 27th, and last, Grand Prix victory of Jackie's career, and came where it mattered most.

Jarama 1974

Jarama saw the beginning of the Lauda–Ferrari legend. After the 1973 season, one of the very worst in Maranello history, the team had been completely revamped. After four years with Ferrari, Jacky Ickx had left to go to Lotus, and Clay Regazzoni, following a desultory season with BRM, returned. The Swiss was asked to suggest a second driver, and he proposed Niki Lauda, who had been with him at BRM, similarly frustrated by the unpredictable carryings-on of Mr Louis Stanley. When the offer came Niki decided to forget his contract with the British team, and no one – save, perhaps, Big Lou – was terribly surprised.

From the start of their association, Lauda, Regazzoni and Ferrari jelled effectively. Although Clay was nominally the team's number one, it quickly became apparent that Niki was going to be the pacemaker. This state of affairs was not new, of course, and has frequently been a source of strife down the years, but Regazzoni, never a man weighed down with too high

Lauda followed by Regazzoni and Ickx, 1974 Spanish Grand Prix

an opinion of himself, accepted the situation with equanimity. There was never the slightest dissension between the two. Before the start of the 1974 season they tested incessantly, and by the time it began Ferrari was rising from the ashes.

At Jarama Lauda and Regazzoni started first and third, with Ronnie Peterson's new Lotus 76 between them. It was a dismal day in the Madrid region, but began to clear a little as noon, race time, approached. For all that, everyone went to the grid on rain tyres, and Ronnie's gripped best away from the line. After one lap he led from Lauda, Regazzoni and Ickx. This was Peterson at his best, leading for the sake of it despite the fact that his Cosworth-engined car was far less manageable in the rain than the silky smooth flat-12-engined Ferraris.

After half an hour the rain had stopped and the track was quickly drying. In these new circumstances wet tyres began to come apart and soon the pit lane was in a state of chaos. On this occasion, though, the comic opera came not from the Italians but from Lotus. While the Lauda and Regazzoni tyre changes were expertly and swiftly carried out, Peterson's was slow and Ickx's disgraceful. The Belgian, who had recently beaten

Lauda in the rain at the Race of Champions, had high hopes for Jarama, but he was sent on his way with a rear wheel still loose, and he got only as far as the end of the pits before stopping.

Jacky switched off, awaited attention. When the offending wheel had finally been tightened, he pressed the button – and was instantly doused in white fire extinguisher mist! After that, the two buttons were moved further apart . . .

Both Lotuses eventually suffered with overheating problems, a consequence of running harder than expected while the radiators had been partially blanked off with masking tape. And after the black cars had gone, Niki and Clay had not the slightest opposition, the red cars droning round endlessly until two hours had passed and the thing could be stopped.

It was in no way a memorable race, save that it brought Niki Lauda his first Grand Prix victory. Afterwards he joyfully accepted the trophy. The unsentimental Austrian, we know, has no time for such outward trappings of success, but that particular cup sits on the desk in his study . . .

McLaren mechanics with an M23

Österreichring 1974

Carlos Reutemann was one of the most complex individuals ever to sit in a Grand Prix car. His driving was sometimes sublime, but occasionally he squandered his almost boundless natural talent by surrendering to the moment. The only predictable aspect of Reutemann the racing driver was that, throughout his career, he would keep you in suspense. You never knew whether this weekend he would drive off into the distance or fade into midfield obscurity.

In 1974 he dominated four times with the Brabham BT44, but won only three Grands Prix. In Argentina, where victory would have meant most, the car let him down in the last laps, and he was never to come so close to a home victory again. But in South Africa, Austria and America he was in a class of his own.

The victory at the Osterreichring was perhaps his best of the season. Lauda, still charging in those days and in front of his own people, took pole position,

Carlos's final attempt to wrest it being foiled by an oil slick from Fittipaldi's McLaren in the closing minutes. No-one, however, had any doubts as to who was the quickest man at the track.

In the enormous heat of race day Reutemann made a perfect start and beat Lauda up the hill in the Hella Licht Kurve, at that time a flat-in-fifth corner. Thereafter Niki put Carlos under the fiercest pressure, but never quite managed to get by. It was, in fact, the Ferrari which wilted, but Clay Regazzoni continued the good fight for Maranello, with Fittipaldi, Peterson and Pace right behind him.

Reutemann's performance was perfect that day. It had pace and determination and also a good deal of intelligence. As early as eight laps into the race a dark stripe appeared on the Brabham's left front tyre. Carlos therefore altered his cornering technique to give the tyre an easier time, and he somehow contrived to do that without compromising his lead.

The rivals fell away, with all manner of problems. In the closing laps, under no threat whatever, Reutemann eased a little but still won by almost a minute.

A year later Carlos and the Brabham were back in Austria. They qualified 11th, and finished 14th . . .

Paul Ricard 1975

In 1975 Niki Lauda and the Ferrari 312T came together to produce one of those partnerships from which legend springs. Fourteen races made up the World Championship, and the Austrian started nine of them from pole position, winning five. A glance at the record book suggests virtual domination, but that was not quite the way of it. True, there were races, such as those at Monaco and Zolder, where he faced no serious

Tyrrell under wraps

Lauda pursued by Scheckter, Hunt and Mass, 1975 French Grand Prix

challenge, but at other times he had a World Champion's luck riding with him – the momentum of the season, if you like. At Anderstorp he and the Ferrari were off the pace, yet lasted and won. And the French Grand Prix at Paul Ricard was not without moments of worry.

Lauda was not feeling good when he arrived at the bland and dusty circuit. A recent bout of influenza had left him weak and lethargic; not until the last practice session did he demoralise everyone by snatching a comfortable pole position . . .

On the face of it, Niki's main opposition was going to come from Jody Scheckter's Tyrrell and James Hunt's Hesketh, second and third on the grid. Lauda made a great start and braved it out with Jody into the first turn, from which he emerged in front. It was as well that he did, for it had a crucial effect on the outcome of the race.

After a single lap Lauda and the Ferrari led by two seconds, and their advantage grew steadily for half a dozen more. For the rest, the problem was Scheckter, the head of an increasingly lengthy snake . . .

Two years earlier Jody, then very much a novice

Grand Prix driver, had led most of the way in a McLaren, and he decided to set up the Tyrrell in the same way, with very little rear wing. That way, he figured, no one would be able to get him on the mindless mile-long straight, and he could hold them all back through the tight corners. The policy worked, but Messrs Hunt, Mass, Fittipaldi and the rest did not appreciate it. James finally got by after eight laps, by which time Lauda – and his slipstream – were six seconds up the road.

Perhaps the real story of Ricard in 1975 was that Mass drove possibly the best race of his life, demonstrating an aggression rarely seen before or since. In the McLaren M23 he passed Scheckter and completely outshone his team leader, Fittipaldi. Once clear he began, gradually, to reel in Hunt's Hesketh. And together they started to close in on Lauda . . .

The Ferrari was in trouble, understeering more with every lap, but Niki knew exactly how much he could pay out – 'One minute or one second . . . same nine points!' Over the line a couple of seconds covered the three of them. It was another Sunday in a Lauda summer.

Österreichring 1975

An unaccountable day. More than most circuits, the beautiful Österreichring is unforgiving of mistakes. More than at any other time, mistakes are made in the rain. More than most drivers, Vittorio Brambilla made mistakes. More than most teams, March were unsuccessful in Grand Prix racing. And yet . . . in torrential conditions, Brambilla's March won the Austrian Grand Prix, a victory against the run of play, if ever there was one.

Carved into the foothills of Styria, the Österreichring is constantly at the mercy of unpredictable weather. There is no middle ground. For the Austrian Grand Prix there is either blazing heat or monsoon, sometimes both.

Race day in 1975 seemed to have found a compromise. The morning was bright, but not oppressively hot. But the skies then caught the mood of the race. During the morning warm-up Mark Donohue crashed his Penske March at the flat-out Hella Licht Kurve, the car clearing the guardrail and hitting advertisement scaffolding beyond. Brought back to the pits, and

thence by helicopter to hospital, the American looked to have had a miraculous deliverance, hurting but in one piece.

Later in the day came the news that he had suffered a brain haemorrhage and was unlikely to survive. As word began to circulate, so the clouds gathered and blackened in a Wagnerian gesture. As race time aroached, the drivers stood around anxiously. Even in perfect conditions, the Österreichring is a spooky place. In terms of lap speed, it virtually matches Silverstone, but here the accent is on long, sweeping curves rather than straights. As was frequently the case at Spa, an accident tended to have serious consequences, and Donohue's disaster was a very recent reminder. No one relished the thought of racing there with the added problem of poor visibility.

The rain, when it came, was devastating, but finally it abated. Everyone went to the grid with wet tyres, but there seemed a chance, just a chance, that the odd patch of blue might win the day. After a few laps that hope was washed away, more rain falling with an increasingly

ferocious intensity.

In the early laps Lauda led in his Ferrari, this being the year when Ferrari led everything and won most. But in the really atrocious conditions Niki began to fall away, being replaced at the front by Hunt's Hesketh, which had Brambilla and the March right behind.

Vittorio looked the whole way like a man on the verge of an accident, but he pressed on with courage and adrenalin, and when James was held up by his tardy team-mate, Brett Lunger, the Italian spotted what he thought might be a gap and went for it. Astonishingly, he got through.

For ten laps the orange March skated round in the lead, pulling away easily from the Hesketh, but could Vittorio keep it all together for 54 laps? In the end, there was no need. Conditions were now impossible, with cars slithering off the road everywhere, so officials decided to halt the race, and Brambilla was given the flag. The Italian and his 751 had been highly competitive throughout the season, completely dominating – until retirement – in Sweden, and running on the pace

virtually everywhere. But no one expected the combination actually to win. . .

As he went over the line a disbelieving Vittorio suddenly realised that he had won a Grand Prix. He was wildly, ecstatically joyful, and violently waved his arm in salute.

It was a mistake. At 225 kmh (140 mph), the March began to go sideways, and then spun, once, twice, several times . . . people in the pits heard the flat sound of breaking fibreglass somewhere up the road, and saw an orange blur coming off the guardrail.

Two or three minutes later Brambilla was back, the 751 – astonishingly – tattered but still mobile. Out of the cockpit climbed the stocky victor, and never was a man so happy! No shrug, no blasé, bored, been-there-before grin. For Vittorio, winning was something new, and at 37 that meant something. Fingers and thumbs refusing to cooperate, it was some time before the Moët et Chandon cork came free. When it did, Brambilla used the bottle like a fire hydrant. This was his day, and he never had another like it.

Jarama 1976

The circuit of Jarama, on the outskirts of Madrid, was constructed on the site of one of the bloodiest battles of the Spanish Civil War, and perhaps its ghosts live on. In its short life as a Grand Prix venue, Jarama has witnessed a tremendous amount of controversy and unpleasantness, which reached a peak in 1980, when the 'manufacturers', such as Renault and Ferrari, withdrew from the event, which eventually lost its World Championship status.

In 1976, too, there was drama, and perhaps it was here that Grand Prix racing's massive political problems had their beginnings.

The row began after the race. It had been a good Spanish Grand Prix, with Niki Lauda, in considerable pain from broken ribs, straining to keep his Ferrari ahead of James Hunt's McLaren. Ultimately, the Austrian lost the battle, Hunt taking the lead at half-distance and keeping it to the flag.

Carlos Reutemann

At post-race scrutineering, however, the McLaren was found to be 1.8 cm too wide, and Hunt was disqualified forthwith. A tough decision by the Technical Committee of the CSI (now FISA), but straightforward. Certainly the infringement was minute and almost certainly caused by tyre bulge, but rules are supposed to be absolute. Later in the year, for reasons best known to itself, the FIA Court of Appeal reinstated Hunt as the winner of the race.

Quite right, too, said McLaren's Teddy Mayer (an erstwhile lawyer!). *Being disqualified was like being hanged for getting a parking ticket!* Well, yes, he had a point, but so too did those who claimed that being a little bit illegal was like being a little bit pregnant. The lines were clearly defined . . .

Forgetting the dissension, there was much to applaud at Jarama. Both Hunt and Lauda drove magnificent races, as also did the late Gunnar Nilsson, who took third place with his Lotus. And there was a splendid dice for fourth place.

At Jarama Morris Nunn produced his new Ensign N176, and it was surely the most attractive and elegant car in the place. At the wheel was Chris Amon, returning to Formula 1 for one last season. The New Zealander knew all about Jarama. As long ago as 1968 he had started on pole position in a Ferrari, had dominated the race until . . . a fuel pump fuse had blown.

Amon qualified the new Ensign in tenth place, directly in front of the works Brabham-Alfa Romeos of Pace and Reutemann. However, both out-accelerated him on the run down to the first corner. Thereafter he struggled with both for the duration of the race, finally finishing between them, in fifth place. A little over a second covered all three.

An odd battle, this, with Amon's grossly under-financed little car taking on Bernie Ecclestone's biggest and best. Reutemann stuck grimly to the task of keeping the Ensign back, but he loathed the Brabham-Alfa Romeo and never understood Ecclestone's decision to take on the Italian engines after so many successes with Cosworth. At the end of the season he moved to Ferrari, by which time Amon had finally given up Formula 1.

Monaco 1976

There was never any real doubt that Lauda was going to win, but that was the story of the mid-1970s. He had won the World Championship conclusively in 1975, and had started his defence of the title in remarkable fashion. The five races had gone thus: first, first, second, second, first. He had won at Monaco the year before, and now he was on pole position again. It was one of those days when Niki sat out most of the final session, utterly confident of his position. Next up were Regazzoni's Ferrari, Peterson's March and the Tyrrell six-wheelers of Depailler and Scheckter.

At the start, though, there was a flurry of excitement, for Ronnie succeeded in splitting the Ferraris on the drag down to the first corner! Could this be a challenge to Lauda? Outrage!

After only a couple of laps the answer was clear: even the acrobatic Peterson, using all the verve at his command, was being dropped. He could stay ahead of Regazzoni without problem, but ahead was a machine within a machine. It did not go wrong. Calmly, and with no apparent dash, Lauda pulled away a little more each lap.

The picture changed somewhat on lap 25, when Hunt, who had been running at the back after a spin, suffered a major engine blow up, the McLaren instantly putting down a lot of oil. Regazzoni found it, had a long and lurid moment which allowed both Tyrrells past, and then so also did Peterson, who went off backwards at Tabac, wrecking the rear end of the March. The race – what race there was – was over.

In the late stages there was rain, but everyone stayed out there on slicks, and Lauda pressed on, completely untroubled. It was less straightforward for Clay. After his debacle on Hunt's oil, the Swiss had been flying along in angry pursuit of the Tyrrells. With 14 laps left, the surface slippery, he had passed Depailler and now, with just five to go, he was gaining very swiftly on Scheckter. But . . . at the fatuously tight Rascasse, the Ferrari's inside front wheel clipped the barrier, throwing the car into a spin. Tyrrell could relax again.

Lauda, still moving along easily, won by a little over ten seconds after another uncanny demonstration of routine superiority. As usual, it left the rest a bit nonplussed.

Brands Hatch 1976

In the summer of '76 England was in the grip of Hunt fever. Wherever you looked there was a picture of him, this man with the scruffy clothes and the Public School accent. In the contrived atmosphere of Hesketh Racing his popularity had been considerable, but only when he joined McLaren and started winning regularly did the real adulation begin. It was to burn out quite quickly, but for a while it was of astonishing intensity.

James came to Brands Hatch just a fortnight after winning the French Grand Prix at Paul Ricard, and had established himself as the season's only real rival to Niki Lauda. Already it seemed that the Austrian's second consecutive World Championship was a mere formality, but Hunt at least promised to spice up the second half of the year. And at Brands the crowd had its hopes of him, almost daring him to lose.

In practice he kept the faith, qualifying on the front row, just a fraction slower than the inevitable Lauda. Hot

Hunt passes Lauda into Druids, 1976 British Grand Prix

sun. A massive crowd. Tension. At the green light Niki got away slightly better than James, but Clay Regazzoni was quicker on the move than either. As the cars went into Paddock for the first time, the two Ferraris were side by side – and suddenly there was mayhem. They touched, Regga's car spinning sideways, directly in front of Hunt's McLaren, which rode over the Ferrari's rear wheel, flew into the air and almost flipped. Also involved were Chris Amon's Ensign and Jacques Laffite's Ligier. Lauda, unscathed, had meantime gone on his way . . .

The race, of course, was stopped, which delighted Hunt. He had gingerly set off again after the accident, but knew that his car's steering was seriously damaged.

The rules at that time stated that if a race was stopped a driver could not restart in a spare car. Sensibly, therefore, the McLaren mechanics immediately set about repairing James's damaged M23. Even so, there seemed the distinct threat that the crowd's hero would not be allowed to restart, and soon they made it clear that this would not be acceptable to them. For a few minutes it could have been Monza, a great wall of sound booming from the grandstands, together with a hail of beer cans. Perhaps fearing a riot, the Stewards announced that, yes, James was in the race . . .

He drove a beautiful race. *In the early stages I just couldn't stay with Niki because I had appalling understeer on left-handers. But the handling got better and better as the fuel load lightened, and then I began to feel confident. I couldn't believe how good a job the mechanics had done. When I caught Niki finally, soon after the halfway mark, we were lapping consistently in virtually the same times we had done in practice! It felt fantastic, really, and I knew I was going to win, just knew it . . .*

On lap 45 Hunt took Lauda into Druids, and the Austrian made no real attempt to fight back. For the remaining 40 minutes the spectators purred contentedly in the sunshine, revelling in James's smooth progress towards the flag. At the finish Lauda was 16 seconds behind. Hunt was mobbed.

Ferrari, however, protested the victory, claiming that the McLaren had been stationary – and therefore out – when the 'first' race was stopped, an assertion vigorously denied by James and his team. Several weeks later, the FIA Court of Appeal found for Ferrari, and awarded the race to Lauda. The drivers' close friendship survived intact, but Hunt's undisguised animosity to Maranello remains.

Monza 1976

Monza '76. Even now, years later, memories of that weekend are clear and sharp. The Anglo-Italian war, which had been simmering for much of the season, finally overflowed into open conflict, and the weather provided an appropriate backdrop to all the dissension. There was turmoil at Ferrari, for the crowd knew that Regazzoni was to be replaced by Reutemann, and did not like it. And, towering above everything else, there was Niki Lauda, back from the dead.

Six weeks before, the Austrian had crashed at the Nürburgring, and initially there were serious doubts that he would survive, but then came the stories that the worst was over, that he was recovering swiftly. Even so, few believed that he would be seen in a racing car for a long time, if ever. And now here he was, dreadfully scarred but willing to climb aboard once more.

It rained hard throughout the first day of practice, but Saturday, thankfully, was dry, if dull and overcast. In these conditions Jacques Laffite's Ligier set the best time, fractionally ahead of Jody Scheckter's six-wheeled Tyrrell. Pace and Depailler made up the second row, and then, fifth, was the extraordinary Lauda, comfortably quicker than the other *Ferraristi*, Reutemann and Regazzoni.

The trouble began that evening. Earlier in the day the organisers had taken random samples of fuel from various teams in the pits. Analysis showed that the McLaren and Penske teams had petrol which was over the maximum octane level. Therefore, said the organisers, their Saturday times would be disallowed. Their grid positions would be based on their times of the day before – which, of course, had been wet . . . James Hunt, Jochen Mass and John Watson started from the back, to the undisguised delight of the crowd.

Another grey and forbidding day dawned, but it remained dry until the racing was finished. Scheckter snatched the lead on the first lap, and came by with Laffite, Depailler and Peterson behind him. Lauda was 12th at this point, but very quickly began to cut back through the field. Even at this early stage, though, it was obvious that Maranello honour was in the hands of Regazzoni, who quickly dispensed with Reutemann and moved up to join the leaders.

Ten laps into the race Ronnie went by Jody, and it was a matter of waiting for the March to break, which it always did. Patrick Depailler soon went past Scheckter as well, and then so did Regga and Laffite. For now the miseries of the weekend were forgotten. This was turning into a very fine race. First National City, who

Peterson had won his only Grand Prix for March, and Regazzoni had kept the faith with his adoring public, causing them to question even more fervently why he was being shown the door when his replacement had finished a distant ninth.

Most of all, though, the crowd wanted Lauda that day. In the circumstances of the time, the Austrian's drive must stand as perhaps the bravest in the sport's history. In the last few laps, running fourth, he had seen

Six-wheeled Tyrrell

had done a deal to sponsor Peterson's March only that morning, were certainly getting value for money. As the race went on, it was obvious that Ronnie had the measure of everyone, although in the last few laps Clay put in one of his celebrated charges.

There was little more than two seconds between them at the flag, and afterwards everyone – apart from the McLaren and Penske personnel – was happy.

the Ferrari's oil pressure dropping and eased off so that he was almost caught on the line by Scheckter. But he made it, just 20 seconds behind the winner, and the true magnitude of his achievement was only seen afterwards as he gingerly removed helmet and bloodied balaclava. No, he had not won, but there are some defeats more triumphant than victories.

Peterson, Depailler and Regazzoni, 1976 Italian Grand Prix

Silverstone 1977

James Hunt was reigning World Champion when he came to Silverstone in 1977, but the heady days of the previous season were beginning to fade from the memory. He had stolen the title from Niki Lauda with a remarkable series of drives, but had won nothing since, apart from an inheritance at the Race of Champions where Mario Andretti's Lotus 78 had retired in the late stages.

In the middle of the 1977 season the American was the man in ascendancy, for the 78, Formula 1's first 'wing car', had set new roadholding standards. At the French Grand Prix, a couple of weeks before Silverstone, Andretti had won, passing John Watson's faltering Brabham-Alfa Romeo halfway round the final lap. For the British Grand Prix, though, Mario was less

confident, for the Lotus's major shortcoming was its very poor straightline speed, vitally important on the long Northamptonshire straights.

John felt good about his chances. The dramatic, brutish-looking BT45 handled beautifully, and no one doubted the horsepower of the flat-12 Alfa. Reliability was another matter, of course, but Watson nursed the belief that eventually everything would come together for him.

His opposition at Silverstone came from a frankly unexpected source, for Hunt put the McLaren M26 onto pole position, beating the Brabham-Alfa by a quarter of a second. The M26 was one of those cars which had to be dragged into competitiveness. At no stage did it turn into corners well, and all who drove

it found its steering unacceptably heavy. Hunt, fortunately, had the physique and stamina to cope with that, and he found the car very much more at its ease through the fast sweepers of Silverstone. A year earlier he had 'won' the British Grand Prix at Brands Hatch, only to be disqualified later. This was a race he particularly wanted.

The day was memorable, with glorious weather, a massive crowd and a great race. Watson got away to perfection, but Hunt, troubled by a clutch which refused to free properly, was slow off the line, and found himself behind Lauda's Ferrari and Scheckter's Wolf before reaching Copse for the first time.

John made the most of his chance, and came by at the end of lap one with an impressive lead. Behind him, James quickly disposed of Jody and began to catch the Ferrari for second place, but Niki was enjoying himself and driving hard. Not until lap 23 did Hunt assert himself, into the Woodcote chicane. The crowd braced itself for a battle: here were the two leading British drivers running one and two in the British Grand Prix . . .

For 26 laps Watson and Hunt ran nose to tail in perfect stalemate, but then, almost inevitably, James came by alone. A few seconds later the red Brabham-Alfa burbled into the pits. A fuel pressure relief valve had broken. No one could remember that happening before – but, of course, it had to happen to John . . .

The remaining laps were a cakewalk for Hunt, a winner for the first time in many months. But James was magnanimous in victory: *I was delighted to see John go, but I can't pretend I would have passed him. I was handling better than he was, and I think I was a fraction quicker. But getting by was a different matter. My only chance was that he would make a mistake – and I knew that wasn't going to happen . . .*

Disappointed once more, as he was throughout that summer of 1977, John nevertheless felt good about a job well done: *I felt very sure of myself. For me, leading is much easier than following, and I was confident he wouldn't be able to get past. He got alongside me into Woodcote on one lap, but there was no way I was going to give.*

There were three factory McLarens in the race that day. Like Hunt, the team's regular number two, Jochen Mass, had an M26, but there was also an old M23 for a newcomer named Gilles Villeneuve. Comfortably faster than Mass throughout, the young man created a sensation in his first Formula 1 drive. Inexplicably, though, McLaren decided against signing him for the following season. Enzo Ferrari showed more foresight.

Mosport 1977

All in all, the 1977 Canadian Grand Prix was a dramatic affair. A week earlier, at Watkins Glen, James Hunt had taken a decisive victory in the rain, his McLaren M26 finishing ahead of Mario Andretti's Lotus 78. When the circus arrived at cold and grey Mosport Park it was clear from the outset that these two would again be the protagonists of the weekend.

In Canada, however, it was the American who had a decided advantage, taking pole position by more than half a second from James, with Ronnie Peterson's Tyrrell and Gunnar Nilsson's Lotus on row two. Back in 17th place, after finding his car absurdly short of grip, was Gilles Villeneuve, making his debut for Ferrari. The Italian team was in some turmoil at this time. Niki Lauda, having clinched his second World Championship at the Glen, then decided that he had enough of the 1977 season, enough of Ferrari. He therefore flew to Toronto, collected his fee for promoting the race and promptly headed off for Salzburg . . .

The days of qualifying were marred by rows, chiefly sparked by the drivers, who were understandably dissatisfied with the track from a safety standpoint – even if they loved it as an exercise in driving. Adding fuel to the fire was an accident in which Ian Ashley and his Hesketh became airborne over a flat-in-fifth brow. The car cartwheeled down the road, cleared the guardrail and hit the top of a television tower. It looked like an aircraft accident, and Ashley's escape, with only minor fractures, was almost beyond belief.

Race day was one for lumber-jackets and gloves – and also for the Lotus 78, which had little difficulty in working heat into its tyres. Andretti led from the start, but Hunt at once took second place behind him and the two of them quickly went away from the pack, which was led by James's team-mate Jochen Mass.

For most of the race that was the story, Hunt continuing to stalk Andretti, without ever looking likely to get by him. Mass, however, changed the entire outlook of the race. At three-quarter distance he was involved in a tight battle for third place with the Wolf of Jody Scheckter when the leading pair came up to lap them.

Jochen clearly had not the slightest interest in anything around him, other than keeping Scheckter behind. Mario and James got around Jody without difficulty, but Mass was a different matter. Andretti suffered first.

Derek Daly (Ensign) at the Österreichring 1978

Mass really screwed it for me, no question. It seemed like he was offering me space to go by, and then he chopped over in front of me. He'd already held me up enough for Hunt to close up on me, then he damn near took me out of the race. Team tactics, I guess you'd call it – or that's what I thought at the time. That let Hunt past me, but a couple of corners later they had some kind of misunderstanding, and Hunt was into the wall, so I guess Mass was pretty democratic with his blocking . . .

That, indeed, was the way of it. As James moved to go by his team-mate, Mass moved the same way and the cars touched. Hunt's McLaren hit the guardrail very hard and was destroyed, its driver, somewhat agitated by now, then clouting a marshal.

All this left Andretti with a clear run to the flag, with Scheckter more than a lap behind. After 78 of the 80 laps, however, Mario's engine blew up. Jody cantered in for his third win of the season, and the one which mattered more than any other to his team owner, Canadian-based oil millionaire Walter Wolf. For Mosport Park, it was the end of the Grand Prix road (the following Canadian GP was held in Montreal).

Kyalami 1978

What made me so mad was that Chapman had three gallons of gas taken out of my car on the grid! I didn't really argue with him because the guy was nearly always right. But he was just paranoid about weight, and it cost him dearly so many times. 'Colin,' I says to him, 'if I run out of fuel, I'll take it out on your hide.' 'Trust me,' he says . . .

If Mario Andretti had lost the World Championship by fewer than nine points in 1978, it would have been for the want of those three gallons. Had his car not stammered into the pits with three laps to go, he would assuredly have won the South African Grand Prix. Fortunately for Colin Chapman, Mario anyway went on to take the title comfortably.

The American shared the front row with Niki Lauda's

Ricardo Patrese in the 1978 Arrows

Brabham-Alfa Romeo, and took the lead from the start, trailed by Jody Scheckter's Wolf. In the early going it looked like an Andretti-Lotus walkover, but at quarter-distance Mario noticed that his left front tyre was starting to blister, and decided to sit back for a while. Scheckter took the lead, but was soon displaced by Riccardo Patrese and the Arrows A1.

This was only the second race for Jack Oliver's new team, and it looked for all the world as if Patrese were going to win it. The Italian quickly built up a sizeable lead, with Patrick Depailler's Tyrrell moving up to second, followed by Lauda, Scheckter and Andretti. Mario's team-mate, Ronnie Peterson, had qualified poorly and run most of the race in midfield, but was up to seventh by half-distance.

In the closing stages it began to look as though Andretti's wait-and-see policy was going to pay off. One by one, those ahead ran into trouble, with Scheckter spinning off and Lauda's engine blowing up. With 15 laps left, Patrese's engine also expired, the car having run like no Arrows ever has since. That left Depailler in the lead, with Andretti, his car working superbly now, catching him. Third, behind Mario, was Ronnie.

Even when the livid Andretti came in for fuel, Patrick was doomed. His tank also was running dry, his engine misfiring, and now Peterson took up the chase. As they went into their last lap Ronnie was gaining, the Lotus virtually on the Tyrrell's tail as they came out of Crowthorne.

This victory was going to be important to someone. After nearly five years of Formula 1 Depailler had still to win his first Grand Prix. And Peterson, back with Lotus after a desolate time with March and Tyrrell, was keen to show the sceptics that he was the man of old.

Round that last lap they ran, sometimes side by side, more than once banging wheels. But Ronnie was very determined to get by, and Patrick's car was hobbled. At the Esses the Lotus 78 slipped ahead, and the issue was settled. From 12th place on the grid, the great Swede won by half a second.

Into the air went Chapman's hat. Andretti, seventh, resisted the temptation to run over it . . .

Peterson and Depailler, 1978 South African Grand Prix

Brands Hatch 1978

For sure it was always an ambition to win the British Grand Prix – particularly at Brands Hatch. A dangerous place, but very satisfying for a driver. When I came to Europe to race Formula 2 in 1970, I went to the Grand Prix as a spectator. Was the race when Brabham ran out of gas on the last lap, and Rindt won. It made a big impression on me . . .

Eight years later Carlos Reutemann did win the British Grand Prix at Brands Hatch, a victory he relished perhaps more than any other. It was unexpected, and it was achieved in richly satisfying circumstances.

Ferrari sparked erratically in 1978, but emerged from the season with a lot of credit. It was the year of the Lotus 79, when ground effect moved Andretti and Peterson into a separate world, these two winning eight Grands Prix between them. Ferrari took five, all but one going to the enigmatic Reutemann.

The Argentine was always absolutely brilliant on his

day, but you never knew when that would be. Add to that the fact that Ferrari were into the first year of an association with Michelin, and here was another quirky element. Sometimes, as at Rio, the French tyres made Maranello dominant, but on other occasions they reduced the Italian team to a state of farce. It had been that way at Paul Ricard, just a couple of weeks before Brands Hatch.

Carlos qualified eighth for the British Grand Prix, nearly two seconds off the pole. However, on this summer day there was a race, for the two Lotuses were soon out. Scheckter's hideous Wolf WR5 led from Lauda's Brabham-Alfa Romeo, Patrese's Arrows and Reutemann's Ferrari. But Jody soon retired with a broken gearbox, and shortly afterwards Riccardo's lurid drive ended with a puncture, leading to wrecked rear suspension. After 40 of the 76 laps, only two men were in

James Hunt's McLaren

Reutemann finds the gap to pass Lauda and Giacomelli (33) at Clearways, 1978 British Grand Prix

contention: Lauda and Reutemann. The gap between them was around four seconds.

That, on past record, looked to be the end of the story. Niki, once in front, tended to stay there. And Carlos' great days were usually of the flag-to-flag type; he had never been known as a fighter. Yet now he began, hair by hair, to close on the Brabham.

There was much at stake. On the surface was victory in a Grand Prix, but such a thing was nothing new to Reutemann. Beneath it lay other factors. Wounds from the past. Scores to settle. For many years Carlos had been a Brabham driver, and his working relationship with Bernie Ecclestone had not ended on a harmonious note. After that he had gone to Ferrari, hired by the Commendatore when it seemed certain that Lauda would not return after his Nürburgring accident. Niki did, of course, and made no secret of his feelings about Reutemann, never missing an opportunity to try and 'psych' him. During their year together, in 1977, the two men were anything but friends.

So here was an additional spur for Carlos. He could win the British Grand Prix at Brands – and at the expense of Lauda and Ecclestone. Onward he came until, on lap 60, the two red cars were together. Passing Niki, however, would be a different thing altogether . . .

Who knows what might have happened had it not been for the intervention of Bruno Giacomelli? The Italian was running seventh in his McLaren, and about to be lapped. At the approach to Clearways the leaders quickly closed on him. Bruno saw them and prepared to let them through on his right, but by this time Niki had already committed himself to the left. As Giacomelli moved that way the Austrian had momentarily to lift. There was a gap on the right, down the inside, and in a move of incisive brilliance Reutemann was through, past and gone. Into Paddock he had momentum on Lauda, and the matter was settled. Niki seemed to lose heart for a few laps and dropped back, but gathered himself together for a last charge. Too late. Carlos was a second and a half earlier to the flag . . .

163

The Brabham 'fan car'

Zandvoort 1978

This was the Year of the Lotus. In 1978 Colin Chapman produced the 79, and the type number of the car reflected its superiority: it was a year – at least – ahead of its time. Only Lotus had a fully operational ground effect car that season, and the 79's cornering abilities moved it into a league of its own.

When you have a chassis that much better than the rest, recalls Mario Andretti, *your advantage kind of snowballs. First of all, the rest of the guys are psychologically beaten before the race even starts. More than that, though, it means that you don't have to drive so hard, you stay fresher and have something in reserve if something goes wrong towards the end, and the same goes for the car. You can change up at lower revs, make the engine live longer, and also the tyres. All these things increase your chances, not just to lead a race but to finish as well. When people asked me about the 79 it was difficult to avoid getting into clichés. There's only so many ways you can say 'fantastic,' but no other word really did the job . . .*

Andretti came to Zandvoort looking for his sixth Grand Prix win of the season. He led the World Championship by nine points from team-mate Ronnie Peterson, and the only threat to his title hopes came from

himself and his car. Ronnie, a man of unfashionable integrity, had agreed, on joining Lotus, that 1978 was to be Mario's year, that he would not try to beat him.

For all that, there was great pressure on Andretti at Zandvoort. Two weeks before, at the Osterreichring, he had crashed on the first lap, and Peterson had gone on to one of his greatest victories. In Holland it became clear that the Swede would leave Lotus for McLaren at the end of the year: in those circumstances, therefore, he had little to lose. *If I were in Ronnie's position, I'd just go for it,* said John Watson in Holland, his sentiments echoed by many of his fellows.

Andretti and Peterson were firm friends, however, and Mario's anxieties came from elsewhere. *Ronnie's word meant something. I wasn't worried about him at Zandvoort. It was just pressure from having the championship hanging over me, the thought that I might have thrown it all away in Austria. Let's face it, if I retired in Holland and Ronnie won, we were equal on points with three races to go. I knew he wouldn't try to beat me – but, on the other hand, if I retired from a race I couldn't really expect him to pull out as well . . .*

They qualified first and second, as usual, with Andretti on the pole, and from the start the two black and gold cars moved smoothly away, maintaining the pattern of the season. Peterson sat right behind Andretti, often giving the impression that he could go by if he so wished, always dropping back into line.

It looked very silky and smooth for them, but reality was different. Ronnie was running out of rear brakes as the race wore on, and Mario's car lost its high-pitched wail with 20 laps left: an exhaust had cracked, and that cost him some revs. *My real worry about that was that it might ignite the rear bodywork. Pieces of fibreglass were coming apart there and hitting Ronnie. Tell you what, though, if it had ignited, Ronnie would have had one big fire*

to follow for a long time – I wasn't stopping while that car had life in it . . .

They kept going, crossing the line for what seemed like just another Lotus 1-2, one of several in 1978. In fact, it was the end of a whole chapter of Grand Prix racing. At Monza, a fortnight later, Andretti won again, but was penalised a minute for allegedly jumping the start. After the race, however, he knew that his World Championship was assured. Ronnie, his only rival, had crashed within seconds of the start, and during the night he died.

When that happened, I couldn't have cared less about the championship, Mario remembers. *Nothing else mattered.* He stayed with Lotus for two years more, but never won another Grand Prix.

Interlagos 1979

Man, it was a rude shock, I'll tell ya. I guess we'd cleaned up so much the year before that we figured it would simply continue into '79. In Argentina those Ligiers were just so much quicker it

was a joke. Gone. Then we went on to Brazil, to Interlagos where we'd tested during the winter. Reutemann and I really gave it a go in qualifying – and we finish up third and fourth! It

was the same thing . . . we couldn't get near the goddam Ligiers. They'd come up with their first ground effect car, and out of the box it just plain jumped over us . . .

Mario Andretti was not the only driver shaken by the early form of the Ligier JS11. After three erratic seasons of Formula 1 the French team had abandoned the venerable Matra V12 engine (although not, as it turned out, for good), turning instead to 'standard issue' Cosworth DFV power. They had studied the all-conquering Lotus 79, learned good lessons and designed a car with tremendous downforce. And they had decided on a two-car team for the first time, Patrick Depailler joining Jacques Laffite as equal number one – a scheme for which Jacques had limited enthusiasm . . . A degree of 'needle' between the drivers, however, served only to amplify the capabilities of a remarkable new Formula 1 car.

I was not particularly concerned about Patrick joining Ligier, Laffite recalls, *but I made it clear from the start that I thought we should have a number one and a number two – whichever way round they wanted it. But no way should we have had two number ones – and I think time proved me right. I had not too much trouble with Patrick in the early races, in South America, but by the time we got to Belgium, for instance,*

we were racing for the lead as if we were in different teams. And so we ruined our tyres, and threw the race away . . .

Laffite had won conclusively in the JS11's debut race in Argentina, with Depailler fourth, delayed with fuel vapourisation. At Interlagos they again monopolised the front row of the grid. They ran first and second from beginning to end, finishing way ahead of the rest.

Why was it so easy at that time? Even now Laffite has no idea. People who say it is a black art, they are right. In Brazil I set my pole position lap on normal race tyres and with the fuel tanks half-full! No problem. Hardly any adjustment necessary to the cars after Buenos Aires. Get in, go! Maybe that was the problem. We were quick – very quick – and we did not really know why. We just thought we had the best car ever built, and it would be quick everywhere, but no . . . and when we were off the pace, it was the same thing: we did not really know why! During the season we began to test all the time, with different cars and all kinds of modifications. We lost our way, went round in circles, confused ourselves. Eventually we tried to go back to the beginning, set the car up exactly as it had been in South America – and we could not do it. Still, it was good while it lasted. In Argentina and Brazil, you know, winning was so easy I couldn't believe it . . .

Dijon 1979

Jean-Pierre Jabouille and Renault won their first Grand Prix in 1979, appropriately enough at Dijon, before a home crowd, where it mattered. Their great sadness, though, is that no one remembers the race for that reason. Everyone's attention was focussed elsewhere, fifteen seconds back down the road.

Dijon-en-Prenois, abounding in fast corners and with a steep uphill haul towards the end of the lap, is a circuit where horsepower counts for more than anything else. During qualifying the Renaults of Jabouille and René Arnoux qualified first and second, and on sheer speed only one man seemed likely to worry them: Gilles Villeneuve, third fastest with the Ferrari T4, half a second clear of the next man.

Race day brought perfect turbo weather, the great heat of the practice days giving way to cool greyness, overcast skies. The massive crowd began cautiously to hope. The only chance of a French victory this day was the yellow of Renault, for Ligier, previously splendid that year, had confused themselves as usual, and the cars' handling was lamentable.

For me, it is very important to have a good start, mused Villeneuve on race morning. *I must at least split the Renaults on the first lap . . .* Typically, the little man was true to his word, catapulting the Ferrari away up the road to begin a stunning opening lap. Quickly he built up a lead of five seconds over Jabouille, with Arnoux way back after a tardy start. After 14 of the 80 laps,

René Arnoux (right) and Gilles Villeneuve duelling for second place in the last few laps of the 1979 French GP

Jabouille on his way to victory, 1979 French Grand Prix

though, René was up into third, and the two Renaults had only a single Ferrari to concern them – albeit in the hands of the world's best driver.

No others figured that afternoon. It was strictly a three-car race, with Villeneuve driving out of his skin to keep the faster Renaults at bay. It was typical Gilles, gallant and awesome in spite of the odds. By half-distance, Jabouille had gained on the Ferrari, and was playing the race like the fanatical fisherman he is, paying out a little, reeling in. Villeneuve, his tyres starting to go away, was on the hook, but prepared to fight to the last.

On the 47th lap Jean-Pierre calmly took the lead on the pit straight, whistling away into the distance. *Once in the lead, I wanted to build up a gap to Gilles, demoralise him, but I could tell when I passed him that his tyres were finished . . .*

In the Ferrari pit they got themselves ready for a Villeneuve tyre change. Jody Scheckter, lapping at nothing like the pace of his team-mate, had already been in for fresh Michelins, but still Gilles stayed out. Nothing could be done about Jabouille, but now second place looked to be coming under threat from Arnoux . . .

The last few laps of the 1979 French Grand Prix beggar description. Relentlessly the Renault closed in on the hobbled Ferrari, and with five laps left the two were nose to tail. Three laps to go, and René went by on the main straight, just as his team leader had done. It was going to be a Renault 1-2, but . . .

When René passed me, I thought he would run away down the straight, like Jabouille, but he didn't. I thought I would get him back as soon as possible, because he wouldn't be expecting it. Villeneuve, in terrible handling trouble with his ruined tyres, rightly reasoned that Arnoux, too, had his problems. The Renault's fuel pick-up was a little awry.

No one really knows how many times those two cars passed and repassed during the last three laps, how many times they banged wheels, slid off the road, rejoined. It was desperate in a manner not seen in Grand Prix racing for many a year, condemned by some as irresponsible, lauded by more as heroic. Asked for his comments later, Mario Andretti, as usual, summed it up best: *Nothin' to worry about. Just a coupla young lions clawin' each other . . .*

After the race, the young lions (Villeneuve–Arnoux was the final order) jumped from their cars, shook hands and embraced after the race of their lives.

And there lay Jabouille's tragedy. In the fastest car in the race he had driven magnificently, finished the race totally exhausted. The winner, French in a French car in France. And nobody was talking about it . . .

Zandvoort 1979

Zandvoort '79 summed up the season in many ways, with a pitched battle between the two fastest drivers – Gilles Villeneuve and Alan Jones – a tremendous drive by Jody Scheckter, and more points for the ever-present Jacques Laffite. From every point of view it was a memorable day.

The second half of the year belonged, in competitive terms, to Alan and Gilles. In the Williams FW07, Jones had the best chassis in the business; in the Ferrari T4 Villeneuve had far less grip, but a little more power. Between the two drivers there was enormous mutual respect and admiration. British downforce versus Italian horsepower: it made for some memorable battles.

Both these men wanted victory above championship points. Thanks to the absurd 'split season' scoring system of the time, Jones could not win the title, for the first half of his season had been marked by retirements. Villeneuve, by contrast, did have a chance, but the World Championship was always a secondary consideration to Gilles. He wanted to win races.

At Zandvoort the Williams and the Ferrari qualified second and sixth, but after a single lap the pattern of the race was set: Jones first, Villeneuve right behind. Scheckter, by contrast, almost melted his clutch on the line, and was 19th! In a couple of laps, though, the clutch began to 'come back' and Jody really got to it. By the tenth lap he was in sixth place!

In the meantime Gilles stalked Alan, taking the lead with a blend of audacity and genius, fighting the Ferrari round the outside of the Williams at Tarzan. The French-Canadian had taken a chance on tyres, opting for a fairly soft compound. At this early stage of the game

Arrows wreckage at Tarzan, 1979 Dutch Grand Prix

they allowed the Ferrari to run with the Williams – but they were also responsible for Villeneuve's downfall. For 35 laps he led, but Jones began to close up. At the exit of the controversial 'Scheckter chicane', designed by Jody, Villeneuve's T4 went into massive oversteer which became a spin.

Now Jones led again, but Gilles quickly collected himself. He had not hit anything, and resumed without losing a further place: *I thought my tyres had gone off, and that was why I spun. As it turned out, my left rear tyre had a slow puncture . . .*

Coming past the pits, at maximum speed, the tyre exploded, Villeneuve expertly spinning the Ferrari to a halt without further damage. The engine was stalled, and we expected to see him throw off his belts and walk home. Instead, to everyone's astonishment, he pressed the starter button, selected reverse, then first, and set off once more! At the end of a remarkably fast three-wheeled lap he brought the car into the pits, its left rear corner trailing along behind.

Jones finally won the race without problem, followed by Scheckter and Laffite. *The race meant a great deal to me,* commented Frank Williams. *Sentimentally it was important, because Piers Courage was killed at Zandvoort in one of my cars. And it was emotionally satisfying, too. When you've been in a battle with that little French-Canadian, you know it . . .*

In the aftermath of the race, opinions of Villeneuve's never-say-die attitude varied. Some thought his behaviour foolhardy and dangerous, others finding it gallant and heroic. The man himself was in no doubts.

Having seen it on TV, I can understand some of the criticism. In fact, on that basis I would even criticise myself – not for coming back on three wheels, because that was no problem. But when the wheel was dragging along, that could have caused an accident for someone else. I understand that, but I had no idea it was there because I couldn't see it in my mirrors. I thought it had gone altogether. If I had known it was there, for sure I would have stopped.

On the other hand, I have no regrets about trying to get back to the pits in the first place. As long as the car will run, I will try to get it back – and I think if you don't do that, you are not a racing driver. My conscience is clear. I don't care what people say about me. I won't change my driving for them . . .

Monza 1979

It was one of those perfect afternoons. If you're lucky, you get maybe half a dozen of them in a whole career. I knew that if I won that race I was World Champion, and my main reason for going to Ferrari was that I felt I had a better chance of the title with them than any other team. So there was this opportunity to do so much in a single race – win the Italian Grand Prix at Monza in a Ferrari, and become World Champion at the same time. The practice days were hell, with all the pressure and interviews and so on, but in the race I had no real worries. Gilles was right behind me all the way, and there was still a chance that he could win the title. But he gave me his word that he wouldn't try to pass, and he had more integrity than anyone else I've ever met . . .

If Jody Scheckter had 'no real worries' during the 1979 Italian Grand Prix it shows what a calm fellow he was in a racing car. True enough, he could rely on Villeneuve to keep to the pact, but there were several cars in the race which were capable of running with the Ferraris, and one or two – notably the Renaults of Jabouille and Arnoux – which were discernibly quicker.

Lauda's Brabham

Jody and Gilles got the start absolutely right, rocketing past the Renault front row to screams of approval from the grandstands. The crowd waited apprehensively, for it is very important to them that a Ferrari should be in front at the end of the first lap. Sure enough, Scheckter's red T4 howled out of the Parabolica in first place. As the Ferrari came up to the line, though, it was apparent that it had a yellow shadow. Arnoux was right behind, and at the approach to the first chicane the Renault went by, stilling the crowd.

Lap 13 brought the end of Arnoux's bid, however, and he retired with a severely misfiring engine. Jody was now back in the lead, with Gilles at his back, and Jacques Laffite's Ligier close enough for anxiety. This was to be one of the Frenchman's greatest drives, but it brought no reward. Soon after half-distance he, too, was out.

Before the race, both Ferrari drivers had seen Alan Jones as their biggest problem. The Australian came to Monza on a streak, having won the last three Grands Prix, in Germany, Austria and Holland. In Italy, however, he was in trouble from the very start, limping away from the line and stopping after five laps for a new battery . . . Once back in the race he drove like the charger he was, lapping at record speeds merely for the sake of doing it. But the stop had cost almost two complete laps.

And . . . there was Regazzoni. Here was one of Monza's all-time favourite heroes, twice a winner for Ferrari in this race, now threatening to beat the red cars! A few days past his 40th birthday, Clay became positively inspired as the race neared its end. On the second lap his Williams had come into contact with Piquet's Brabham-Alfa at the Curva Grande, Nelson pinballing down the road. Piquet finished up, with the monocoque, on one side of the road while the engine was on the other. Regazzoni came out of that unscathed, and then drove hard and fast for the rest of the race. With a couple of laps left, he was but two seconds from Villeneuve's tail.

The Williams, though, was low on fuel, and began to misfire during those last five or six miles. The Ferraris screamed over the line to rapturous applause, and the gallant Clay followed five seconds later.

Ferrari-Ferrari-Regazzoni. Monza could have wanted nothing more. Up on the podium all the months of strain and harrassment had fallen from Jody's face.

I wasn't giving him a present, you know, smiled Villeneuve. *We were both driving hard, I can tell you. No, of course I never tried to pass him . . . I just sat there, hoping like hell that he would break!*

[Months later, when Clay Regazzoni crashed so disastrously at Long Beach, I remembered sadly a touching little ceremony in the Monza paddock during practice. A fortnight before, at Zandvoort, Regga's car had hit Arnoux's soon after the start. There was never a more well-loved man in motor racing, and in Italy the Renault team good-naturedly presented Clay with a birthday present, which turned out to be tragically prophetic. It was a wheelchair, complete with racing wheels and wings and stickers.

Regazzoni knew he was going to lose his Williams drive to Carlos Reutemann. *You're never going to have such a competitive car again,* I said to him at Monza. *You're 40 years old, and you've had a tremendous season. Surely you must have thought about stopping?*

You don't understand why I do this, he replied. *For me, is not necessary to win. I am happy simply to drive, to be a part of racing . . .* The tragedy of Clay Regazzoni is greater by far than any other I have known in the sport.]

Long Beach 1980

Long Beach in 1980 was the scene of Nelson Piquet's first victory and Clay Regazzoni's last race. It was also the place where rival constructors began to feel *really* frightened by the word 'turbo'. René Arnoux and Renault had won the two previous races, at Interlagos and Kyalami, and now the little man qualified his car second at Long Beach. A turbo competitive at a tight street circuit! It was time for a little scaremongering, a little Formula 1 McCarthyism. End of Grand Prix racing as we know it, Turbos under the Bed, that kind of thing. Arnoux's practice lap rattled FOCA's cage.

Impressive as it was, however, the Renault was more than a clear second away from Piquet's Brabham BT49. Gordon Murray, Goodyear and Nelson contrived to put together one of those rare weekends when everyone else is going for second place. From the start of practice the Brazilian was in good shape, for all his dislike of slow, tight tracks, and in the final session no one could get near him.

It was indeed a curious grid. Ferrari, traditionally Long Beach specialists, were nowhere with their recalcitrant T5, with Gilles Villeneuve, utterly dominant in 1979, unable to match his pole time of that year. Third on the grid was the Alfa Romeo of Patrick Depailler, refuting those who had written him off when he smashed his legs in a hang-gliding accident the previous summer. And fourth, just behind him, was something of an embarrassment to most of the aces: Jan Lammers and

Piquet at Long Beach

the ATS. Ahead of Alan Jones and Carlos Reutemann, the Williams pair . . . ahead of most people, in fact.

On race day, though, the ATS was out after but half a lap, and the Renaults' challenge faded with their brakes. Piquet was into an immediate lead, and no one was to emerge as a realistic threat to him. While the Brabham raced away, those behind tripped each other up, with Bruno Giacomelli's Alfa accounting for both Williams cars – in separate incidents! By the end of the afternoon, second and third places belonged to Patrese's Arrows and Emerson's Fittipaldi, well prepared cars well off the pace.

If Long Beach that year launched the hard-nosed Piquet into the ranks of Grand Prix winners, and, a year later, into the record book as World Champion, it stands in the mind of most as the race which left Regazzoni with

appalling injuries. The Swiss, newly back with Ensign after a highly successful season with Williams, had started from the tail of the grid but was up to fourth at three-quarter distance. Long Beach was one of his favourite circuits, and he had won the inaugural Grand Prix for Ferrari four years earlier.

On lap 58 the red, white and blue car rushed into the braking area at the end of Shoreline Drive, but it did not slow to any discernible extent, instead shooting unchecked down the escape road at something over 250 kmh (160 mph). After striking Zunino's abandoned Brabham, the Ensign hit a tyre wall head on, moving back by several feet a concrete barrier beyond. That Clay survived was remarkable, but severe spinal injuries have since confined him to a wheelchair.

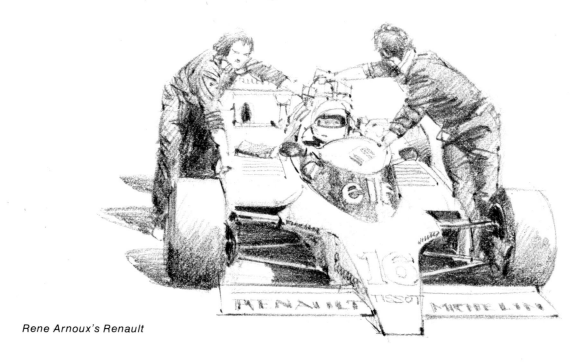

Rene Arnoux's Renault

Brands Hatch 1980

As a race – for the spectators, I mean – I guess it was a great bore. After Ricard, I think people were hoping for another big Williams-Ligier battle, and after qualifying I reckoned they might get it. Laffite and Pironi had a definite advantage at Brands, without a doubt, but in the race the Ligier team defeated itself, as it very often does! Actually, I was pretty grateful when that happened. I don't think I could have done a lot about them, quite honestly . . .

Alan Jones remembers his victory in the 1980 British Grand Prix as one of the easiest of his Formula 1 career. Certainly, it could not have been more opportune, for the Australian came to Brands Hatch with a narrow three-point lead in the World Championship.

A couple of weeks before he had scored perhaps the most satisfying win of his life, defeating the French in France. Alone he had taken on the Ligiers, applied and

sustained pressure to the point that they overheated their front tyres and had to slow. Alan, aggression always triggered by a whiff of garlic, drove faultlessly, afterwards touring the circuit with a Union Jack, relishing the crowd's discomfort . . .

Thus, Ligier were more keen than ever to win in England, to redress the balance, get back their self-respect. In practice the blue cars were demonstrably superior to any others. Didier Pironi taking pole position, Jacques Laffite next up. Then came Jones, team-mate Carlos Reutemann and the Brabham of Nelson Piquet.

Pironi got away beautifully in the race, leading the first lap by two and a half seconds. Behind him trailed Laffite, Jones and Piquet. By the second lap Pironi had extended the lead, and Laffite was going clear of Jones . . .

I really wanted that race, Pironi commented, *but not because of beating the English in England. Nothing like that.*

You cannot go racing simply on emotion. No, I wanted to win because the car was fantastic that weekend, incredible. I felt I could do anything with it – that anything was possible. And also I believe that Brands Hatch is the best driver's circuit in the world. So . . . the pleasure of that car on that track is hard to describe. Something incredible.

At the end of lap 19 Didier came in, nearside front tyre almost flat. All four wheels were changed, and he resumed at the tail of the field, beginning a stunning comeback drive which would take him as high as fifth before suffering another puncture . . .

After Pironi's stop, Laffite led for ten laps before it became clear that he, too, had a puncture, this time in the left rear. At the end of lap 30 he signalled to his pit: in next time. But he never reappeared, the tyre breaking up completely, putting the car off the road. The Ligier challenge was over, and Jones cruised in for a comfortable win.

I think that race really highlighted the difference between the

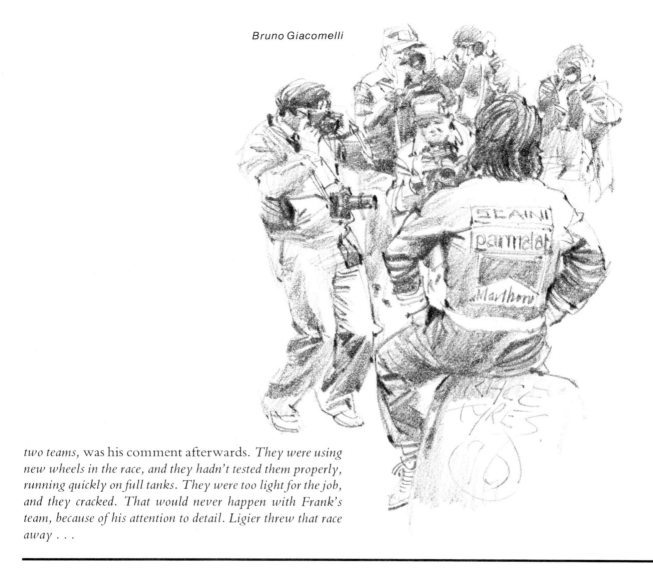

Bruno Giacomelli

two teams, was his comment afterwards. *They were using new wheels in the race, and they hadn't tested them properly, running quickly on full tanks. They were too light for the job, and they cracked. That would never happen with Frank's team, because of his attention to detail. Ligier threw that race away . . .*

Zolder 1980

When they came to Zolder in 1980, the Ligier team felt confident that their car would be competitive. This was their sort of circuit. A year earlier they had dominated the Belgian Grand Prix on sheer pace, yet lost the race through foolishness. Jacques Laffite and Patrick Depailler, instead of working together against the opposition, had fought tooth and nail, overheating their tyres in the process. Depailler had crashed and Laffite, furious, had been second behind Scheckter's off-the-pace Ferrari. This time, said the French, there would be no such mistakes.

Laffite's partner was now Didier Pironi, who proved slightly quicker in practice. Both Frenchmen were beaten to the pole, however, by an inspired Alan Jones, and it looked like a repeat of the year before: Williams versus Ligier.

There was no battle. At the green light Pironi timed everything to perfection, got the drop on Jones and led into the first corner. Behind them came Laffite and Reutemann. That was the order at the end of the opening lap, and it remained that way until past the halfway mark. Didier, in the lead, was making no mistakes, and the expected challenge from Alan never materialised. Forgetting the leaders' pace, it became a somewhat soporific afternoon . . .

Lap 40. Excitement! Drama! Laffite, in brake trouble

with the second Ligier, came in to have the system bled, rejoining afterwards to set the fastest lap of the race. Reutemann, a long way back with intermittent gearbox problems, inherited third place.

In the late stages Pironi's advantage multiplied, for Jones's left front tyre was at the end of its life and the Australian wisely eased off. He was almost a minute behind at the end.

This was Didi Pironi's first Grand Prix victory, and he accepted all the plaudits with cool aplomb. It was no surprise to him. He had always know precisely how good he was, and it was therefore inevitable that he was going to win races.

I knew I had a good lead, and it seemed that Jones couldn't catch me. Therefore it was time to be prudent. It was very easy to win that race, and I should have won more that season. In fact, I believe that I could have won the World Championship if everything had gone the way it should have done. Jacques is a very nice guy, but he always had too much power at Ligier. He tried to manage everything. The car was fantastic at some places, but Jacques made some wrong decisions, and then the team lost its way . . .

Monaco 1981

This one was truly against the run of play. Right enough, Gilles Villeneuve somehow qualified his Ferrari 126C second on the grid (and there were those who speculated that Piquet's 'practice' Brabham, on pole position, might just have been a little lacking in the avoirdupois department . . .), but that was the result of instinctive genius, sheer mind and talent over matter. The Ferrari turbo gave splendid horsepower, but the

chassis was heavy, crude and cumbersome. Even Villeneuve, they said, would be in trouble with it on race day.

To a point, they were right. In the first few laps Piquet pulled out a two-second advantage over the Ferrari. The start of the race had been delayed: there had been a fire at the Loews Hotel, which partly sits on the tunnel through which the cars pass. Considerable quantities of water had fallen — *were* falling – through the roof of the tunnel, right onto the quick line through. A wider line than usual was required, therefore, and the tunnel could no longer be taken flat. This was the fastest part of the circuit, a section where Ferrari horsepower could make amends for Ferrari handling, so now Villeneuve's strong suit was gone.

After 20 laps, the little man was under strong pressure from Alan Jones and the Williams. There was, between these two, an understanding, a mutual respect,

which was extended to no one else. Gilles knew that he could block the Australian indefinitely, but such was not his style. He also recognised that by so doing he would cook the Ferrari's brakes. When Alan catapulted out of Casino Square and dived for the inside line into Mirabeau, the French-Canadian did not cut across. Equally, he gave Jones not an inch more than he needed.

The overtaking done, Alan charged after Piquet. The Brazilian had issued some fatuous threats against him at Zolder a fortnight before, and Jones was out to make a point. When he caught the Brabham, his pressure was merciless, and Piquet's composure began to crumble. As the Williams driver sat back for a breather, Nelson misjudged a lapping manoeuvre and slid into the barrier at Tabac. *I don't often burst out laughing in a racing car,* remarked his laconic rival later.

After a few laps in the lead, though, Alan's high

spirits began to sink. The car was beginning to misfire, and the problem was worsening all the time. His lead over Villeneuve was secure, it seemed, but Gilles had driven hard all afternoon, and was close enough to be a factor. With nine laps to go, Jones made his big mistake. Assuming his problem to be one of fuel vapourisation, he brought the Williams in to be topped up. When he rejoined, the Ferrari, being driven on the limit, was but six seconds adrift – and his misfire problem remained.

As the two of them went into their last five laps, Villeneuve was right in touch, clearly intending to make the pass along the pit straight. Jones, really hobbled now, moved to the right, but Gilles was not to be denied. Alan made it difficult, not impossible. That mutual respect again.

By the time they took the flag, the Williams was 40 seconds behind, its driver disappointed but philosophical. Later in the season, at Hockenheim, the fuel system misfire would recur, robbing him of another victory and, in consequence, another World Championship.

There was delirium for Villeneuve at the finish, for that Ferrari should never have been within spitting distance of victory at a place like Monte Carlo. Three weeks later, he would do it again, at Jarama, and that would be the last win of his life. But Monaco '81 will be remembered, like Montreal '79, as a day when the two stars of the era showed all their greatest skills.

Imola 1981

The first San Marino Grand Prix meeting began acrimoniously, for the previous race, in Argentina, had been won by Nelson Piquet's highly controversial Brabham. There it had been equipped with an ingenious hydraulic suspension system and fixed skirts. According to the rules, skirts were banned, but other teams quickly decided that they must follow the Brabham lead if they were to be competitive. At the same time, the officials at Imola declared firmly that the regulations must be observed. Scrutineering therefore brought problems. On the first morning of practice 'the brothers' went off for a meeting, leaving Ferrari and Renault to learn about Imola.

Ultimately, FOCA's might won the day and all the teams with illegal cars were allowed to race them. But Imola is a power circuit, and Gilles Villeneuve took an easy pole position in an agricultural chassis devoid of the latest tricks. What he had with him was truly awesome horsepower. Former Ferrari team-mate Carlos Reutemann qualified second with an inspired lap in the Williams.

Ferrari practice was a blend of blistering speed and clouds of smoke, their engines expiring with regularity. No one, including the drivers, expected the red cars to last very long on race day.

They were wrong. On a cool, damp afternoon Villeneuve went straight into the lead, with team-mate Didier Pironi slotting in behind him. In drying conditions Gilles led for 15 laps before coming in for slicks. It seemed like the right decision, but no sooner had he

Gilles Villeneuve

rejoined than the heavens opened, which meant another stop – for more wet tyres. Relegated to the back of the field, Villeneuve then began a typically mesmeric drive, the fastest man on the track just for the sake of it.

Pironi had taken over the lead when Gilles stopped, and for a while looked very comfortable at the front. Piquet, in the meantime, had come through well after a bad start, passing Reutemann and Riccardo Patrese and moving up to second place. As the track began to dry out, it was evident that the Brabham was handling very much better than the Ferrari. It was also much kinder to its tyres.

For many laps Pironi grimly defended his lead, but it was obviously only a matter of time before he had to give way. With only a dozen laps remaining, Piquet calmly outbraked the Frenchman, who was in dire trouble by now and slipped down to fifth by the end, passed by Patrese, Reutemann and the second Brabham of Hector Rebaque.

Piquet's victory was the result of an intelligent drive, both forceful and patient as the occasion demanded. From Reutemann's point of view it was a frustrating afternoon, his Williams hobbled by severe vibration, the result of the tyres moving on their rims. At the finish Carlos was third, less than two seconds behind Patrese. By season's end he would lose the World Championship to Piquet by a single point. Bearing in mind the Buenos Aires fiasco, most felt that the title should have gone to Argentina rather than Brazil . . .

Hockenheim 1981

Long before the race finished the hire cars were lined up at the paddock gate, for the Ecclestones and Mayers were looking for a quick getaway. Long gone were the relaxed days of evening prize-giving ceremonies. The prizes would arrive later, figures on a bit of paper.

The chequered flag came down for Nelson Piquet, and within minutes all the weekend's stars were changed and ready to leave. Near the back of the queue was a large Mercedes, for the use of the Williams team. Quite clearly this was an area to avoid. Carlos Reute-

mann, furious about his blown engine and fretful of his diminished World Championship lead, had a noisy and emotional row with an Italian journalist. And then Alan Jones arrived, face like thunder. Twenty feet from the Mercedes, he hurled his leather briefcase into the open boot, then climbed into the back of the car. His expression did not invite conversation.

It was hardly surprising. That day at Hockenheim the Australian had driven one of his greatest races, clearly having the measure of everyone. By aggression

John Watson on the grid for the start of the 1981 Dutch Grand Prix

and guile he had taken his Williams past Prost's Renault and into the lead. As in 1980 he had gone into the final laps of the German Grand Prix in what appeared to be an unassailable position. The year before he had suffered a puncture, eventually finishing third. This time his engine had developed a mysterious misfire, just as it had at Monte Carlo earlier in the year. In both cases the consequence had been a lost victory. But the true damage would not be seen until season's end: with those nine points from Hockenheim Alan would have retained his World Championship.

The race had quickly developed into a straight fight between Prost and Jones, with Reutemann and Piquet hovering in the background. Arnoux's Renault had been removed from the reckoning on the opening lap, limping to the pits with a punctured rear tyre after being clouted by Piquet's Brabham. René rejoined, however, and this had some bearing on later events.

Prost and Jones put on a beautiful display, both men jinking all over the track, the one looking for a way, the other countering his every move. The Renault, surprisingly, did not go away from the Williams dramatically on the long Hockenheim straights. Its rev limiter was cutting in too early.

After 20 laps they came upon Arnoux, who could have helped his team-mate by letting him by on the straight back to the stadium. As it was, he suddenly eased off at the approach to the tight Sachskurve. Prost, not quite sure of his colleague's intentions, slowed slightly before going past on the right, but Jones spotted his opportunity. In a typically incisive move, the World Champion flicked between the Renaults, left his braking to the latest and snatched the lead.

Thereafter, until his engine problem began, Alan pulled away, and Piquet, after adapting well to the loss of part of a skirt, passed Prost for second place. With seven laps to go he also overtook Jones's hobbled Williams. It was a fortunate victory, but an important one, for it ultimately decided the 1981 World Championship.

Long Beach 1982

I must say that I was surprised he decided to come back, said John Watson of his new team-mate in 1982. *He stopped in 1979, but that was predictable because he obviously wasn't enjoying his motor racing at all. Throughout 1981 we heard*

Lauda slips through while Arnoux and Giacomelli collide, 1982 US GP — West

these stories that he was thinking about a comeback, but none of us really thought he would. He drove the McLaren in a test at Donington, and I got the impression that he was disappointed in himself. Formula 1 cars changed a great deal during his absence, and I think the difference shook him. I thought he would go away, think about it, decide against it. But you never know with him. He did come back, and with all the old motivation and application, with something to prove again. He came back a much more dangerous rival than when he retired. There's no doubt about it: he's the old Niki Lauda again . . .

The truth of Watson's words came through clearly at Long Beach. In the first practice session Lauda was beaten only by Keke Rosberg, and towards the end of the last the Austrian seemed certain to start the race from pole position. In the end he was narrowly beaten by the Alfa Romeo of Andrea de Cesaris, but it mattered not. After his fastest lap the youthful Italian was barely coherent, sweating and shaking and weeping with effort and emotion. You saw Niki, cool and unmoved, a few yards along the pit lane, and you knew there was no contest. Pole position, so what? Lauda's expression said it all.

In the race, the story was the same. During the morning Niki had told Andrea precisely what he expected of him. He wanted no foolishness. The Alfa led the McLaren for the first few laps, but always the impression was of a breathless, panting hare trying to keep from the clutches of a wily and loping fox. Held up by a backmarker, de Cesaris shook his fist when he should have been using it to change gear. Lauda was past and gone.

On that warm and breezy afternoon in California the Austrian revived memories of his great days gone by, driving off into the distance with that old insolent ease. Not only the fastest man on the circuit, he was also the smoothest. It was a complete *tour de force*.

Lauda's performance was the antidote to the sickness which prevailed in the pit lane. Grand Prix racing was passing through yet another tedious crisis, with accusations of cheating from all sides. The 'water tanks' controversy was in full spate, Ferrari and Renault accusing the English teams of cheating by running their cars under the minimum weight limit. Not so, said the FOCA boys. We are not breaking the rule, merely deliberately misinterpreting it.

At Long Beach, therefore, Ferrari decided to put the rule book to the test, running the cars of Villeneuve and Pironi with twin, staggered, wings, which extended to the extremities of the car. Each wing was of standard size, and where did it say that only one wing could be used? The Long Beach officials decided that some pieces of misinterpretation were more equal than others, and Gilles's car was disqualified from third place.

But that was petty, squalid, politics. Lauda's drive was something real.

Imola 1982

This was a weekend of controversy, in more ways than one. A few days before the San Marino Grand Prix, a FISA tribunal in Paris disqualified Piquet's Brabham and Rosberg's Williams from their first and second places in Brazil on the grounds that the cars had been underweight. At the same time, motor racing's governing body announced that, in future, the cars' weight would be checked immediately after a race, and that no circumnavigating of the minimum weight regulations would be tolerated.

This was more than some FOCA teams could stomach, and in an act of consummate petulance they withdrew from the race at Imola. More than half the original field, therefore, was gone.

Any fears the organisers may have had, however, were groundless. Ferrari were going to be there, and the *tifosi* care little for the rest. With Didier Pironi and, above all, Gilles Villeneuve to watch, they turned out in their customary vast numbers.

A battle, after all, was in prospect. Imola is a horsepower circuit first, with handling a lesser consideration, and consequently the natural habitat of the turbocharged engine. Renault, with René Arnoux and Alain Prost, would give Ferrari a fight. *FOCA's absence makes little difference here,* remarked Villeneuve after practice. *Apart from Lauda and Rosberg, most of them would have been just traffic . . .* That was a fact that could hardly be denied.

The front of the grid was yellow-red, with the Renaults clearly faster in qualifying trim. But when the 14-car race began, Prost was soon out, and the Ferraris began to pressure Arnoux. Villeneuve it was who did

the work, while Pironi hovered in the background. With 15 laps left, the Renault expired, and the Ferraris were home free, Gilles ahead.

Now began the real story. Maranello team orders decreed that Villeneuve and Pironi hold station, and the French-Canadian duly rolled off the pace, worried about fuel but confident that his team-mate would observe the pit signals. Even when Didier slipstreamed by into the lead, Gilles was unconcerned: it was, after all, a good show for the fans, something for them to watch.

What did concern him, though, was the Frenchman's pace when he was running first. Suddenly, lap times were as quick as when they had been racing the Renault. A little irritated, Villeneuve moved back into the lead, and once more slowed down. *Can you imagine,* he commented later, *how it would have looked if two Ferraris ran out of gas at the end of a race in Italy?*

Pironi, however, clearly had no such thoughts, elbowing past once again, bringing down the lap times, ignoring the advice from his pit. Villeneuve was now furious, though slightly mollified when Pironi let him by on the penultimate lap: *It was stupid of me ... I thought he was being honourable at last, finally observing the team orders.*

Into the last lap they went, Villeneuve-Pironi. Down

187

the straight Gilles was almost cruising, but suddenly Didier was making to go by. Into Tosa, the last overtaking spot on the lap, the Frenchman squeezed through, and Villeneuve was left with no opportunity to respond. In stunned silence, the crowd saw Pironi take the flag first. *There were no team orders, really,* he claimed later. *I thought it was just another race . . .*

A few days afterwards, Enzo Ferrari issued a statement, expressing a measure of sympathy for Pironi, but siding strongly with Villeneuve. It was, however, too late to rescue the relationship between them. *I trust anyone until they break that trust,* said Gilles, *and I will not speak to Pironi again – ever. From now on, it's war. Absolute war.*

Two weeks later, the great French-Canadian was killed at Zolder, going for a time in the closing minutes of the last practice session, trying to work through traffic, holding true his resolution never to lift. The best driver of recent years was gone. He and Pironi never made their peace.

Österriechring 1982

No one really believed that a normally-aspirated car could win at the Osterreichring in 1982. It was confidently expected that this was another circuit to produce a race within a race, an event dominated by the turbos, the rest fighting among themselves. Even if it was hot, even if there were a rash of turbo failures, surely one of them would get through? Who would have put their money on Elio de Angelis and Lotus?

It was my bad luck to join Lotus during one of their uncompetitive phases, said de Angelis. *When I was in Formula 3, Lotus were winning all the Grands Prix, or so it seemed. Colin Chapman always seemed able to give his drivers an advantage, but in three years with him I've rarely had a really competitive car. Often we've been somewhere near the front but I didn't even lead a race until Austria . . .*

Apart from being arguably the most beautiful of the 1982 Grand Prix cars, the Lotus 91 had not made a great impression. Compared with most of its non-turbo rivals it was perilously near the weight limit, and therefore too heavy. And it was not a consistent car, de Angelis and Nigel Mansell finding that its handling characteristics unaccountably changed, sometimes from one practice session to another. *Usually,* recounted Elio, *we'd get to a circuit, go quickly at first, then lose more and more grip as the weekend went on . . .*

Brabham pit stop

At the Osterreichring the reverse was true. De Angelis was fast on the first day, faster yet on the second. True, he was unable to match the time of Keke Rosberg, but the Williams FWO8 was in its very special 'qualifying' trim, and Elio felt sure he could run with Keke in the race. The turbos, of course, were another story.

In the great heat of race day, however, the turbos were in trouble. The Brabham-BMWs of Patrese and Piquet ran away with the early stages, but Nelson was soon in trouble. Riccardo built up a lead, made his planned pit stop for fuel and tyres and rejoined without surrendering first place. Then the Italian's engine seized, pitching the car off the road. That left Alain Prost's Renault at the front, but the French car expired with injection trouble five laps from the end.

From the very start de Angelis had led the rest, quickly assuming a lonely role. Unable to run with the turbos, he was nevertheless beyond the reach of the other normally-aspirated cars. As the Renaults and Brabhams took care of themselves, number 11 moved up the lap charts. And when Prost stopped, the black car took over the lead.

During the last ten laps of the race, though, Rosberg put in a remarkable charge, the Williams perceptibly gaining on the Lotus. As they embarked on the 54th and last lap, Elio and Keke were a second and a half apart, and the 91 surely had it won . . . but de Angelis was starting to suffer from Lotus Disease. His car was low on fuel, and beginning to stutter occasionally.

Round that last lap Rosberg threw himself into a final desperate effort, and dramatic it was, white taking yards off black into every corner. As they emerged from the Rindtkurve, with just a short sprint to the line, the Williams was hidden in the Lotus's slipstream. Judging it so finely that he very nearly clipped Elio's right rear wheel, Keke flicked inside and darted for the flag, but it was all a couple of feet too late. With amazing *sang-froid* de Angelis lifted his left arm in victory, after one of the closest finishes in Grand Prix history. Chapman and the Lotus mechanics were all on the track by this time, a policy which seemed short-sighted when a side by side finish was obviously on the cards. Keke missed them . . .

I hope, said the Finn afterwards, *that I win a race soon. It would be embarrassing to be the first man to win the World Championship without a Grand Prix victory on the way . . .* A fortnight later, his turn came. Another late challenge, this time to Prost's Renault at Dijon. Williams, as usual, were competitive. And Lotus were back to midfield.

Index

*Following in father's footsteps.
Michael Turner's son, Graham,
at Brands Hatch 1982*